LABOR RELATIONS AND PUBLIC POLICY SERIES

REPORT NO. 7

OPENING THE SKILLED CONSTRUCTION TRADES TO BLACKS

A Study of the Washington and Indianapolis Plans for Minority Employment

by

RICHARD L. ROWAN
and
LESTER RUBIN

Foreword by HERBERT R. NORTHRUP

UNIVERSITY OF PENNSYLVANIA

The Wharton School

INDUSTRIAL RESEARCH UNIT

LABOR RELATIONS AND PUBLIC POLICY SERIES

REPORT NO. 7

OPENING THE SKILLED CONSTRUCTION TRADES TO BLACKS

A Study of the Washington and Indianapolis Plans for Minority Employment

by

RICHARD L. ROWAN

and

LESTER RUBIN

with the assistance of

ROBERT J. BRUDNO *and* JOHN B. MORSE, JR.

Published by

INDUSTRIAL RESEARCH UNIT
The Wharton School
University of Pennsylvania

Distributed by

University of Pennsylvania Press
Philadelphia, Pennsylvania 19104

Foreword

In 1968, the Industrial Research Unit inaugurated its Labor Relations and Public Policy monographs as a means of examining issues and stimulating discussions in the complex and controversial areas of collective bargaining and the regulation of labor management disputes. The first four studies in the series dealt with aspects of the National Labor Relations Board and its administration, as will future monographs. The fifth report contained papers read at the fiftieth anniversary conference of the Industrial Research Unit, at which many aspects of labor relations and public policy were discussed. The sixth monograph—*Welfare and Strikes*—was the first empirical analysis of the impact of government payments to strikers on the American collective bargaining system and on the settlements of disputes under that system.

This monograph marks an initial attempt to determine by detailed field analysis what actually occurs when the federal government insists that the skilled construction trades make a serious effort to increase the number and percentage of Negroes in their work force. The study was prepared under U. S. Department of Labor, Manpower Administration Contract No. 82-42-71-76. It examines in detail the situation in two cities—Washington, D.C., and Indianapolis, Indiana. Despite wide variations from city to city in construction practices, it is believed that the information compiled from the experiences in these two cities are sufficiently representative so that the findings have much wider application.

Government efforts to increase minority participation in American industry have developed over the past decade into a system in which federal contractors and subcontractors are required not only to give evidence of nondiscrimination but also to take affirmative action in order to achieve equal employment objectives. The construction industry was singled out for special attention in 1963 with Executive Order 11114.* Executive Order

---

* Exec. Order No. 11114, 3 C.F.R. pp. 774-778 (Comp. 1959-1963).

iii

11246 in 1965 ** further extended governmental influence over equal employment policies by requiring those contractors wishing to do business with the federal government to practice nondiscrimination.

Based upon the powers vested in it under the executive orders and upon experiences gained in St. Louis, San Francisco, and Cleveland, the Office of Federal Contract Compliance (OFCC) in 1967 developed and implemented the first Philadelphia Plan, designed to increase minority utilization in the building trades in the Philadelphia area. This plan was revised in 1969 and upheld by the courts in 1970-1971.***

With the Philadelphia Plan as a model, OFCC began to apply plans in other cities after first allowing local participants to develop their own affirmative action programs. If a particular area developed an acceptable plan, OFCC became a monitor. If the community failed to achieve a voluntary or "hometown" solution, OFCC imposed and administered a plan. The imposed plans always followed hearings designed to determine the crafts to be included and to elicit data for an appropriate set of goals and timetables for those to be covered.

Indianapolis represents a voluntary solution; Washington, an imposed one. Thus this monograph treats examples of both approaches.

The current controversy over quota arrangements in such areas as minority employment make this study particularly timely. To be sure, the authors are not directly concerned with the issue of whether either voluntary or imposed plans to increase minority employment in the construction industry are quota arrangements, or whether the goals set forth in such plans are more than semantically different from quotas. The authors do demonstrate that increased minority employment in skilled construction trades has occurred both as a result of the imposed Washington Plan and of the voluntary Indianapolis one. The authors also provide ample evidence that the threat of an imposed plan provides a powerful incentive to make voluntarism work, but that the conditions are not always propitious to permit a voluntary solution, and they offer carefully considered practical proposals to improve the workings of both volun-

---

** Exec. Order No. 11246, 3 C.F.R. pp. 339-348 (Comp. 1964-1965).

*** *Contractors Assn. of Eastern Pennsylvania* v. *Shultz*, 311 F. Supp. 1002 (E.D. Pa. 1970); affirmed, 442 F. 2d 159 (3rd cir., 1971); cert. denied, 404 U.S. 854 (1971).

tary and imposed plans. It would appear, therefore, that before current programs are condemned, declared illegitimate, or found wanting for any reason, those who would eliminate them are duty bound to offer substitute arrangements which contribute to the solution of underutilization of minorities in construction at least as well as have current arrangements.

The reader should bear in mind that although both plans studied in this monograph have as their goal increased minority participation in construction, the specific goals of each plan are quite different. The Washington Plan sought to secure a representative number of minority man-hours, for particular crafts, on federal construction sites; the Indianapolis Plan had as its goal the enrollment of a proportionate number of minorities in each craft union, or in special training programs leading to union membership. It is difficult, therefore, to compare the two plans as to short-term goal achievements. The reader would do better to evaluate each plan separately as to its long-range implications for true minority participation in the trades and the effectiveness of the methods used to implement each plan's goals, while giving due regard to the environment in which each plan operates.

Professor Richard L. Rowan, the principal author of this monograph, largely designed the research methodology for the total project and personally did most of the field work and research pertaining to Indianapolis. He was assisted by John B. Morse, Jr., who received his MBA degree in May 1972 from the Graduate Division of the Wharton School, and is now working in private industry. The research in Washington, D.C., was under the general charge of the undersigned, but specifically directed by Lester Rubin, a doctoral candidate at the University of Pennsylvania and a Research Associate on the Industrial Research Unit staff. The bulk of the Washington field work was done by Robert J. Brudno, who also received his MBA from the Wharton School in May 1972, and is now working in private industry. Three other graduate students, Kenneth Bridges, Malcolm Pryor, and Wayne Williams, also worked on the project.

Many other persons contributed their time and knowledge and gave shape and substance to this study. The authors would especially like to thank Dr. Howard Rosen, Director, Ellen Sehgal, and Joseph Epstein of the Office of Research, Manpower Administration for helping to make this work possible. Special thanks are also due John Wilks, former Director, Philip J. Davis, Acting Director, OFCC, and their staffs for their help. In Washington, the District of Columbia Manpower Administration, especially the apprenticeship services, has been extremely helpful as have been all the contractor associations, union representatives, and community organizations. Their desire for anonymity will be respected.

In Indianapolis, special thanks are due Herman Walker, former Director, Albert Butler, present Director, and the entire staff of the Indianapolis Plan for Equal Employment. Dr. Emma Lou Thornbrough, Professor of History, Butler University, provided valuable background information. The unions and the contractor associations of Indianapolis, both union and nonunion, all gave freely of their time and knowledge.

The authors wish to thank Miss Mary T. McCutcheon, Mrs. Louise P. Morrison, and Mrs. Judy Campbell for typing, and Mrs. Margaret E. Doyle, Administrative Assistant, Industrial Research Unit, for her usual competency in caring for the numerous details associated with this study. Also, our thanks go to Miss Elsa Klemp and Mr. Michael Johns for their statistical help. Miss Mary Hindman edited the manuscript and indexed the monograph. The authors are solely responsible for all factual content and conclusions contained in this study.

HERBERT R. NORTHRUP, *Director*
Industrial Research Unit
The Wharton School
University of Pennsylvania

Philadelphia
September 1972

TABLE OF CONTENTS

PAGE

FOREWORD iii

PART I: INTRODUCTION AND OVERVIEW

CHAPTER

I. INTRODUCTION 3

Research Methodology and Problems 5
Scope and Purpose 6
Issues and Questions 6
Methodology 8

II. NEGROES IN CONSTRUCTION: AN HISTORICAL PER-
SPECTIVE 10

Craft Differences 11
Trowel Trades 11
Carpentry, Painting, and Operating Engineer
Trades 12
Electrical, Plumbing, and Mechanical Trades 14

PART II: WASHINGTON, D.C.

III. NEGROES IN CONSTRUCTION: THE HISTORY IN WASH-
INGTON, D.C. 19

From Reconstruction to the New Deal 19
The New Deal to the 1960s 22
The 1960s to the Present 25
Summary 31

vii

CHAPTER   PAGE

IV. THE EVOLUTION OF THE WASHINGTON PLAN 32

     Community Role and Official Action 33
         The Hearings 37
         Negotiations and Plan Imposition 39
     The Washington Plan 42
         Requirements of the Washington Plan 45

V. WASHINGTON PLAN DATA ANALYSIS 49
     Apprenticeships 50
     METRO Employment 59
     Minority Man-Hours on Federal Sites 64
     Union Membership 69

VI. THE WASHINGTON PLAN IN PRACTICE: PROBLEMS AND
         PROGRESS 73

         The Compliance Process 74

     Community 76
         The Washington Area Construction Industry Task
             Force 76
         Other Community Agencies 78
         The Urban League 78
         PRIDE and OIC 79
         The Demand for Labor-Community Response 80
         Demand vs. Supply: Continuing Problems 82
         A New Coalition 85

     Industry 88

         Contractor Associations 88
         Union Contractors 89
         Nonunion Contractors 92
         Minority Contractors 96
         Unions 97
         Project BUILD 101

CHAPTER

PAGE

Government --- 104

    Compliance Administration --------------------------------- 104
    OFCC Philosophy --- 106
    Washington Plan Review Committee ------------------ 107
    Bureau of Apprenticeship and Training --------------- 110

  Conclusion --- 110

PART III: INDIANAPOLIS, INDIANA

VII. NEGROES IN CONSTRUCTION: THE HISTORY IN INDI-
ANAPOLIS, INDIANA --- 113

    1800-1920 --- 113

      Education --- 113
      Politics and Civil Rights --------------------------------- 114
      Economic Growth and Development ------------------- 115

    1920-1940 --- 116

      Education --- 116
      Politics, Civil Rights, and Economics ------------------- 118

    1940-1960 --- 120

VIII. THE EVOLUTION OF THE INDIANAPOLIS PLAN ------------- 123

    The Plan and Its Development ------------------------------- 123

      Building Trades Council --------------------------------- 124
      Contractor Associations --------------------------------- 124
      The Black Coalition and Community ------------------- 126
      The Employment Task Force ------------------------------- 127

    The Plan and Its Administration ------------------------------- 129

      Administrative Committee --------------------------------- 130
      Operations Committees --------------------------------- 130
      Indianapolis Plan Staff --------------------------------- 131

CHAPTER

PAGE

Development of Supplemental Agreements 131
An Overview: Fall 1970-Spring 1972 133

IX. THE INDIANAPOLIS PLAN: AN EVALUATION 135

Analysis of Placements 135

A Look into 1972.... 137

Qualitative Analysis 137

The Administrative Committee 137
The Coalition/Indianapolis Plan Staff 140
Staff Operations 142
The Operations Committees 144
Tripartitism of a New Kind 148

Specific Craft Problems and Complexities 150

National Ironworkers and Employers Training Program 150
The Carpenters 153
Bid Conditions 156

Federal Agency Review 158

The Nonunion Sector 162

Other Training and Upgrading Problems 164

JOBS—70 165

X. VOLUNTARY PLANS: IMPLICATIONS AND RECOMMEN-
DATIONS 166

The Government's Role 166

Administrative Organization and Problems 167

Concepts and Flexibility 167

Role of the Black Coalition 169

Communication 169

Union Membership and the Time Frame 170

CHAPTER   PAGE

PART IV: FINDINGS AND RECOMMENDATIONS

XI. FINDINGS AND RECOMMENDATIONS 173

    Findings: The Washington Plan 174

        Administration and Structure 174
        Community 176
        Contractors 177
        Unions 179
        Government 180
        Other 182

    Findings: The Indianapolis Plan 182

        Administration and Structure 182
        Community 184
        Contractors 185
        Unions 186
        Government 187
        Other 189

    Recommendations 189

INDEX 194

LIST OF TABLES

TABLE   PAGE

1 Unions Affiliated with the Building and Construction
  Trades Department, AFL-CIO 4

2 Washington Plan. Negroes in Construction Trades, 1900... 21

3 Washington Plan. Male Construction Employment by
  Race, District of Columbia, 1900-1960 26

4 Washington Plan. Participating Organizations in the
  Washington Area Construction Industry Task Force.. 33

5 Washington Plan. Percentage Minority Representation in
  D.C. Building Trades 43

6 Washington Plan. Percentage Minority Utilization Ranges
  Under Washington Plan 46

7 Washington Plan. Washington, D.C. Apprenticeship Referrals and Acceptances by Craft and Race, January
  1968-May 1971 51

8 Washington Plan. Washington, D.C. Apprenticeship Referrals and Acceptances by Craft and Race, June
  1969-May 1970 52

9 Washington Plan. Washington, D.C. Apprenticeship Referrals and Acceptances by Craft and Race, June
  1970-May 1971 53

10 Washington Plan. Washington, D.C. Apprenticeships:
   From Testing to Employment Sponsor, by Race, January 1968-May 1971 54

11 Washington Plan. Washington, D.C. Apprenticeships:
   From Testing to Employment Sponsor, by Race, June
   1968-May 1969 55

12 Washington Plan. Washington, D.C. Apprenticeships:
   From Testing to Employment Sponsor, by Race, June
   1969-May 1970 56

TABLE   PAGE

13 Washington Plan. Washington, D.C. Apprenticeships:
      From Testing to Employment Sponsor, by Race, June
      1970-May 1971 _____   57

14 Washington Plan. Washington, D.C. Apprenticeships:
      From Testing to Employment Sponsor, by Race, Oc-
      tober 1970-May 1971 _____   58

15 Washington Plan. Average Monthly Employment on
      METRO Construction by Craft and Race for Quarter
      Ending April 1971 _____   60

16 Washington Plan. Average Monthly Employment on
      METRO Construction by Craft and Race for Quarter
      Ending July 1971 _____   61

17 Washington Plan. Average Monthly Employment on
      METRO Construction by Craft and Race for Quarter
      Ending October 1971 _____   61

18 Washington Plan. Comparison of Correlation Coefficients
      of Regression Analysis between METRO Employment
      and Apprenticeship Referrals and Acceptances for
      Selected Trades _____   63

19 Washington Plan. Minority Manpower Utilization on Fed-
      eral Construction Projects Reported by All Contract-
      ing Agencies to OFCC, Quarter Ending April 1971 ____   65

20 Washington Plan. Minority Manpower Utilization on Fed-
      eral Construction Projects Reported by All Contract-
      ing Agencies to OFCC, Quarter Ending July 1971 ____   65

21 Washington Plan. Minority Manpower Utilization on Fed-
      eral Construction Projects Reported by All Contract-
      ing Agencies to OFCC, Quarter Ending October 1971__   66

22 Washington Plan. Overall Progress of the Washington
      Plan as Reported to the Washington Plan Review
      Committee by OFCC _____   67

23 Washington Plan. Union Membership by Race, 1971 _____   70

24 Washington Plan. A Comparison Between Minority Rep-
      resentation in Washington, D.C. Construction Locals
      and Minority Utilization on Federal Projects in the
      Washington SMSA _____   71

25 Washington Plan. Minority Participation in Nonunion Construction, Washington SMSA 92

26 Indianapolis Plan. Population of Indianapolis by Race, 1860-1970 117

27 Indianapolis Plan. Urban-Rural Distribution of Indiana Negroes, 1900-1960 118

28 Indianapolis Plan. Estimated Union Membership of Indianapolis Building Trades, by Race 125

29 Indianapolis Plan. Minority Goals by Craft 133

30 Indianapolis Plan. Minority Placements by Craft, 1970-1971 136

31 Indianapolis Plan. Minority Placements by Craft through September 1972 138

PART ONE

Introduction and Overview

CHAPTER I

Introduction

The construction industry in the United States employs 5 to 6 percent of the nation's labor force and contributes, with its input of labor and materials, approximately 14 percent of the total gross national product. Since a large portion of the labor involved is skilled, craftsmen employed in construction comprise about 13 percent of all skilled hourly employees.[1] Moreover, the industry is often the training ground for skilled employees who find work in manufacturing, utilities, transportation, and the services. Obviously, if minorities are to achieve equality in the workplace, they must share in skilled construction work.

The construction industry has many unique characteristics, not the least of which is the power of the unions. Organized on a craft basis, some eighteen unions (Table 1) exercise control over segments of the industry to a degree rarely achieved by their counterparts in manufacturing. This is in part attributable to the casual nature of the work—employment endures only as long as the job lasts, and the typical construction worker may be employed by many concerns during a year. The unions act as employment agencies and have gradually won control over hiring and training as a result. To enhance their position further, the labor unions have enrolled lower supervision—foremen, general foremen, and even superintendents—in their ranks, thereby taking over what are managerial employees in most industries.

Union hegemony has been additionally enhanced by employer fragmentation and work pressures. Although the industry boasts some large concerns, most contractors are small and financially weak, with entry and exit from the industry frequent. Moreover, the contractors are divided by craft specialties and work together reluctantly. They are also under great pressure to avoid stoppages, for time is money in the industry, and can quickly make the difference between profit and loss. Thus union power is rarely matched by employers. Any study of minority employment in this industry must give major attention to union policies for they clearly dominate employment practices.

[1] Daniel Quinn Mills, *Industrial Relations and Manpower in Construction* (Cambridge: MIT Press, 1972).

TABLE 1. *Unions Affiliated with the Building and Construction Trades Department, AFL-CIO*

National Union	Total Membership	Percentage in Contract Construction
Asbestos Workers	12,500	95
Boilermakers	140,000	n.a.
Bricklayers	149,000	100
Carpenters	800,000	75
Electrical Workers (IBEW)	875,000	19
Elevator Constructors	14,450	100
Engineers, Operating	330,000	75
Granite Cutters	2,843	n.a.
Ironworkers	162,006	74
Laborers	474,529	84
Lathers	15,500	100
Marble Polishers	8,659	83
Painters	200,569	n.a.
Plasterers	68,000	99
Plumbers	284,707	85
Roofers	22,811	100
Sheet Metal Workers	100,000	n.a.
Stonecutters	1,900	n.a.

Source: U.S. Bureau of Labor Statistics, *Directory of National and International Labor Unions in the United States*, 1967, Bulletin no. 1596 (Washington, D.C., 1968).

Reproduced from D.Q. Mills, *Industrial Relations and Manpower in Construction*, (Cambridge: M.I.T. Press, 1972), p. 19.

Another factor of great importance is the significance of local practices. To be sure, national union policies are important factors, but negotiations are largely on a local basis, and practices, including racial employment practices, vary from locality to locality.

Paradoxically, although unions are the key force in the industry, they represent a minority of workers. Most housing construction is done on a nonunion basis, as is much small construction. Moreover, in some areas, particularly the South, the unions are generally weak. Unions are very strong in the construction of highways and streets and all types of large buildings, both public and private, and among the electrical and mechanical crafts. Since the federal government funds a majority of the heavy construction, directly or indirectly, and since its policies through prevailing wage setting have been favorable to unionized construction, it is most appropriate that federal policies also be concerned with effectuating equal opportunity therein. It is also important, however, that the nonunion sector be considered in any analysis since it may well be this sector which employs the bulk of the black construction workers. This study attempts, with only limited success, to include the nonunion sector in its research and findings.

RESEARCH METHODOLOGY AND PROBLEMS

Washington, D.C. and Indianapolis, Indiana were selected as the focal points of this study because they are sizable cities, yet not too large for examination, and have substantial black populations. In both cities, governmental programs to expand minority employment are in effect. The former provides an example of an imposed plan, the latter of a voluntary one. The fundamental differences in approach and philosophy of these plans will become apparent in subsequent chapters.

In Indianapolis, the plan required an increase in the absolute number of blacks employed in the covered trades, whereas in Washington, the plan required an increase in minority man-hours as a percent of total man-hours worked. For this reason, a comparison of the relative success of the two plans is difficult to make. In addition, however, the communities proved quite different in structure and local conditions, and the plans quite different in administration. Research methods utilized in this study reflect these differences.

For example, considerable time was necessary to locate key data sources for Washington. In contrast, such data were readily available in Indianapolis. New hires could be directly attributable to the Indianapolis Plan because complete recruitment, referral, and follow-up records are maintained at a central location. Thus, evaluation of the placement results of that plan is relatively simple. Determination of placements directly attributable to the Washington Plan, however, proved much more difficult. Our attempts to compile such information required hundreds of man-hours of work and cannot be considered in any way complete. Such data, although seemingly vital to determine the success or failure of the Plan, are scattered among government agencies, community organizations, and individual employers. Furthermore, it was not easy to identify a single reason for hiring a minority member in Washington since efforts by community groups, other government agencies, and progressive moves by the industry and unions must be considered.

The primary purpose of this study is to examine the effectiveness and impact of construction affirmative action plans by using two such plans as models. An impartial outsider's look has been taken at the Washington Plan, a model for imposed programs, and at a voluntary, hometown solution in Indianapolis. Aided by our findings and recommendations, policymakers will hopefully be better equipped to chart the government's course in achieving social goals through regulation of the contracting process.

The particular plans selected for study point out different approaches to the same problem. Our research will suggest a generalized technique for evaluating similar plans elsewhere. Conditions unique to each city, however, will be outlined in order to caution those who might seek universal standards of success.

The criteria used to evaluate success or failure are many and are outlined below. In both cities the number of new minority placements in construction employment is an obvious indicator of success. But other factors may be equally important, especially in the case of Washington, where direct cause-and-effect relationships are hampered by scattered data sources. Changing attitudes and policies among those who control employment in the construction industry, as well as the degree of cooperation found in industry, labor, and community relations are two additional considerations. Increased advertising, contact between industry and community organizations, union membership for blacks, lateral entries, apprentice registrations, and other statistical indexes further document the impact of imposed or voluntary plans. In Washington, of course, the man-hour statistics provided by the Office of Federal Contract Compliance are frequently used as a measure of plan effectiveness. In sum, it will be shown that a combination of qualitative and quantitative analyses rather than pure statistics should yield a fairly reliable evaluation of each plan.

Mere collection of data does not provide a reasonable measure of effectiveness if effectiveness is defined to include more than the achievement of numerical goals. Since both the Washington and Indianapolis Plans were designed to have an impact upon job structure, labor supply, the black community, and other variables, qualitative as well as quantitative responses to the following issues and questions were sought:

1. How can jobs won through Department of Labor action be assessed?

2. What is the source of new black hires? Were they already in the labor market, were they trained, or were they imported?

3. What has been the effect of the plan on traditional ways of minority entry into the industry?

4. Is there a lack of Negro candidates for skilled jobs and if so, why?

5. Is the community sufficiently organized to provide the minority manpower necessary to meet plan goals?

6. How well has the plan been publicized in the community? Is it viewed as a beneficial move by the government?

7. How great is the effect of poor schooling, inadequate skills, or limited work experience on minority applicants? Is transportation a significant bar to the inner city youth seeking employment in the suburbs?

8. What have been the effects of other programs which purport to assist in accomplishing the purposes of the plans?

9. How effective is community pressure? Do coalitions or other organized pressure groups exist?

10. Will minority contractors provide the manpower needed to meet plan goals?

11. Has there been a permanent impact on the local construction industry? What has been the impact on minority contractors?

12. Has the plan made an impact on minority attitudes toward the desirability of work in construction? Does construction offer long-range employment opportunity for the minority worker?

13. What impact might new construction techniques in the industry have on black employment? Are, for example, new technologies threatening the jobs in crafts in which Negroes are concentrated?

14. Is the heavy office and light manufacturing construction that is now moving to the suburbs union or nonunion? What impact does such movement have on black employment and the success of affirmative action plans?

15. How transferable are affirmative action techniques and programs into other industries?

16. How much is the nonunion sector affected by these plans?

17. Do nonunion contractors hire the blacks denied membership in unions? Does the lack of strict craft lines prevent enforcement of imposed plans?

18. What effect does international union policy have on local hiring policy? How effective have national training programs been?

19. What informal means of racial exclusion still exist?

20. Does an effective data collection and enforcement mechanism exist?

21. Is compliance consistent and rigorously carried out by contracting agencies?

22. What constitutes good faith effort?

23. How flexible are the plans; do labor, industry, and the community have a meaningful input?

Methodology

As noted earlier, our research design is twofold: data collection and preparation and qualitative documentation in response to the above issues and questions. Quantitatively, construction employment data for Indianapolis and Washington have been collected and analyzed. The data for Indianapolis cover all construction in the city since the inception of the Plan. In Washington, the data relate primarily to the construction of METRO, to all apprenticeship activity registered with the U.S. Department of Labor, Bureau of Apprenticeship and Training (BAT) and with the municipal apprenticeship services, and to minority membership in local unions. These data will document employment changes occurring since the inception of these plans.

Qualitatively, interviews were conducted with government officials, labor representatives, contractors, contractor associations, community representatives and organizations, and men on the job. In this way, our data are brought into proper perspective and answers developed to appropriate questions. To provide general background, the following chapter gives a brief listing of black construction worker problems, and the sections on both the Washington and Indianapolis Plans provide listings and data for Negro employment in construction in those areas over the years.

CHAPTER II

Negroes in Construction:
An Historical Perspective

Negro slaves did the basic construction work in the pre-Civil War South. For many years thereafter, they dominated the southern industry, but in most cases gradually lost out to white workers.[2] There were several reasons for this. First, the whites, in competing for work, frequently used unions as an exclusionary device to further their work opportunities at the expense of blacks. Second, white contractors often favored men of their own race, but few Negroes were in a position to employ men of their race. Finally, training and educational opportunities were highly discriminatory. This was especially true in the newer trades—electrical, plumbing and mechanical—which developed in the intensely bitter Jim Crow era of 1890-1910. Negroes were virtually excluded from learning these trades. As late as 1947, when International Harvester Company built a plant in Memphis, Tennessee, it found that the segregated Negro vocational schools gave no instructions in sheet metal, steamfitting, plumbing, or similar trades which had long been taught in the white vocational schools.[3]

If, however, the South practiced discrimination, the North featured exclusion. Professor Northrup's study of the early 1940s found that Negro craftsmen journeying above the Mason-Dixon line were often barred from work in the North even if they had union cards, while in border cities, like Washington, D.C., discrimination was intense and exclusion the rule.

---

[2] This background is based largely on Herbert R. Northrup, *Organized Labor and the Negro*, (New York: Kraus Reprint Co., Edition 1971), Chapter II.

[3] Robert Ozanne, *The Negro in the Farm Equipment and Construction Machinery Industry*, The Racial Policies of American Industry Series, No. 26 (Philadelphia: Industrial Research Unit, The Wharton School, University of Pennsylvania, 1972), p. 33.

CRAFT DIFFERENCES

Within the industry, different trades have reacted differently to racial problems. Different attitudes toward the utilization of black workers emerged in these three classifications: the trowel trades; the carpentry, painting, and operating engineer trades; and the electro-mechanical trades. A study of each group brings a different perspective to the current problems of minority employment in the building trades.

Trowel Trades

The trowel trades—bricklaying, plastering, and cement finishing—have historically admitted blacks to their journeyman ranks.

> A larger proportion of Negroes are found in the trowel trades than in any other building crafts. This is primarily the result of conditions surrounding the entrance to these trades. Negroes find little difficulty in obtaining employment as hod carriers or as tenders to bricklayers and plasterers. In due course, many "pick up" enough of a particular trade to become "graduated artisans." [4]

The quote refers to the early 1940s but, as Northrup notes, Negroes have been admitted to these trades since pre-Civil War days.[5] Spero and Harris made the following comments concerning the ante-bellum South:

> The plantations were to a large extent self-sustaining units which did practically all their own repairing and made a large proportion of their own supplies. The masters found it easier and cheaper to have their slaves trained in carpentry, masonry, blacksmithing, and the other mechanical trades than to depend upon outside free white labor.[6]

This practice made it impossible for organized labor to ignore the Negro in the building trades. Marshall indicates that

> shortly after the Civil War . . . white bricklayers in New Orleans struck for higher wages but ignored the Negroes who acted as strikebreakers. Thereafter Negro and white bricklayers in New Orleans formed a united front and have one of the most successful

---

[4] Northrup, *op. cit.*, p. 38.

[5] *Ibid.*, p. 17.

[6] Sterling D. Spero and Abram L. Harris, *The Black Worker* (New York: Atheneum, 1968), p. 5.

histories of racial harmony on an integrated basis of any union in the South.[7]

While the bricklayers did not ignore the Negro, they did provide, in some instances, for separate locals. It should be understood, however, that this never became national policy. Northrup notes that

> in 1903, the national officers were strong enough to induce their constituents to amend the union constitution to give the executive board power to grant a charter to a local group if the objection of the subordinate union to the establishment of a second local was based on race, nationality, or religion. This provision was supplemented by a second one providing that a "fine of one hundred dollars shall be imposed on any member or union who shall be guilty of discrimination. . . ."[8]

The history of Negroes in the plastering and cement finishing trades is even a bit more favorable than in the bricklayers' union. Fewer instances of separate locals can be documented and in many cases, Negroes dominated in mixed locals. "Insofar as race discrimination is concerned, Negro plasterers and cement finishers have less difficulty than do other colored building craftsmen."[9] In more recent times the trowel trades still represent the easiest road for blacks to take in the building trades.

Carpentry, Painting, and Operating Engineer Trades

This group of crafts represents a middle position. Entry for blacks has not been as easy as with the trowel trades but it has not been as difficult as in the electro-mechanical trades.

> The carpenters' union has never made exclusion of Negroes a national policy, nor has it confined them to an inferior "auxiliary" status. In 1886, only five years after its founding, it claimed fourteen locals composed exclusively of Negroes in the South. By 1900, it was able to report a Negro membership of 1,000, again mostly in the South. During the next decade, twenty-five additional Negro locals were added, principally, it appears, through the efforts of a colored organizer employed by the national office.[10]

---

[7] Ray Marshall, "The Negro in Southern Unions," in Julius Jacobson, ed., *The Negro and the American Labor Movement* (New York: Doubleday & Co., Inc., 1968), p. 134.

[8] Northrup, *op. cit.*, pp. 38-39.

[9] *Ibid.*, p. 43.

[10] *Ibid.*, p. 27.

Northrup points out, however, that it became policy for the carpenters to segregate the races into separate locals and that the numerical strength of the white chapters allowed them to obtain greater control over the distribution of available work.[11]

Because the home building segment of the industry is largely unorganized, Negro carpenters tended to be concentrated on residential projects and on repair and maintenance jobs.[12] In the last decade, the separate local system was abandoned and serious attempts to integrate Negroes were made. Today there are a sizable number of black union carpenters.

"The policies of the painters resemble in many ways those of the carpenters. Negro membership was encouraged before 1910, and colored organizers were used for that purpose. Interest in fostering Negro membership then fell off . . . ." [13] Like the carpenters, Negro painters have worked on residential, maintenance, and alteration work, again a fact attributable to the failure of the painters to organize this sector of the industry. Separate locals have now been largely integrated.

Although Negroes were never barred from membership in the operating engineers' unions, widespread discrimination has existed:

> The question of a color bar in the membership requirement of the operating engineers' union arose only at one convention. The issue was debated in 1910 when a southern local advocated a "white only" clause. The color bar was rejected on pragamatic grounds. The union was then essentially a stationary engineer's organization with no control of the labor supply. The Negro engineers could not be excluded from employment. Therefore it was considered preferable to include them in order to control them. Negro members of stationary locals are not uncommon today, but they are rare in hoisting and portable locals. The matter has remained in local hands, and there is no doubt that considerable discrimination exists. Until racial discrimination became a widespread issue in the nation and in the labor movement, the international union developed no policy in the matter. As the issue has grown hotter, international officers have begun to warn local unions of possible problems from external sources in the future if discrimination is not ended. Beyond this, the international has taken no action.[14]

---

[11] *Ibid.*

[12] *Ibid.*, p. 34.

[13] *Ibid.*

[14] Garth L. Mangum, *The Operating Engineers* (Cambridge: Harvard University Press, 1964), pp. 232-233.

The history of the operating engineers' trade indicates that blacks were allowed to work in lower status stationary engineering positions but not in the operation of heavy equipment. In addition, the operating engineers' union did not historically take the lead in furthering civil rights. More recently, the national union has sponsored a large number of training programs for blacks, but key locals in California, New York, and Philadelphia have been either charged by federal agencies or found guilty by the courts of discrimination against blacks.

Electrical, Plumbing, and Mechanical Trades

The electrical, plumbing, pipefitting, sheet metal, and iron work trades are those which have been most exclusionist, with few Negroes traditionally admitted to the unions, or even to training opportunities.

> Most exclusionist of the larger building trades unions is the plumbers and steamfitters. To it must go a major portion of the blame for the failure of Negroes to obtain a better representation in this craft.[15]

The plumbers found it to their benefit to exclude helpers from the job and the union. In this way their job empire was protected and scarce opportunities were reserved for journeymen. State and municipal licensing requirements provided the means to enforce this policy. Plumbers' union members are usually part of the licensing boards and in this way can severely restrict new entrants. Even today few Negroes are found in the plumbers' union.

The Negro met with the same restrictions in the electrical trade. The trade has been mostly white since its beginning at the turn of the century. Although there are instances of Negroes in the trade, most efforts of Negroes to join the union have been unsuccessful.[16] The combination of licensing laws and national apprenticeship standards once made it virtually impossible for Negroes either to enter the trade through union membership or to gain any training experience. The union has recently become more open, although local discrimination exists.

Of the other major unions in this group, the sheet metal workers probably rank first on the present discriminatory scale.

---

[15] Northrup, *op. cit.*, p. 23.

[16] *Ibid.*, p. 25.

Although there are variations locally, few organizations have stood so steadfastly throughout the country against increased opportunities for minorities. On the other hand, the iron workers, despite local discriminatory practices, have adopted a progressive training program for minorities and have made serious attempts to implement the program.

Despite national trends, local practices vary considerably and always have. Consequently, our analyses of the Washington and Indianapolis plans are preceded in each case by a more detailed history of black construction employment in these cities.

PART TWO

Washington, D.C.

CHAPTER III

Negroes in Construction: The History in Washington, D.C.

Prior to the Civil War, blacks in the South and, to a certain extent in the border states, were skilled tradesmen in the building crafts. Slave owners found it economical to train and employ black carpenters, masons, and mechanical tradesmen.[17] Many blacks were superior mechanics by the time slavery was abolished in Washington.[18] Whites began to force blacks into more menial tasks, however, as ingrained prejudices perpetuated beliefs that blacks were unreliable and unable to learn technical skills. Without an opportunity to gain experience, young blacks could not develop skills to compete with whites.[19] Efforts by Frederick Douglass and others to help Negroes prepare themselves to "build as well as live in houses" proved ineffective in holding back the inevitable isolation from traditional vocations.[20]

FROM RECONSTRUCTION TO THE NEW DEAL

After gaining freedom in 1865, the black worker began to inherit "Negro jobs" as he was virtually excluded from new industrial opportunities.[21] New electro-mechanical trades emerged, but training and experience were denied to the black man. Gunnar Myrdal notes that after the Civil War, heavy construction,

---

[17] Sterling D. Spero and Abram L. Harris, *The Black Worker* (New York: Atheneum, 1968), p. 5.

[18] Edward Ingle, *The Negro in the District of Columbia*, Johns Hopkins University Studies in Historical and Political Science, Herbert B. Adams, ed., 11th Series, Vol. III-IV (Baltimore: Johns Hopkins University Press, 1893), p. 12.

[19] Arnold Rose, *The Negro in America, 1850-1925: A Study in American Economic History* (New York: Harper and Row, 1948), p. 102.

[20] Charles H. Wesley, *Negro Labor in the United States* (New York: Vanguard Press, 1927), pp. 60-61.

[21] Maurice R. Davie, *Negroes in American Society* (New York: Whittlesey House, McGraw-Hill Book Company, 1949), p. 87.

which offered experience in more advanced techniques, was monopolized by whites and Negro contractors were rarely able to get work.[22] Black contractors still face the circle of no experience without work, but no work for the inexperienced.

In the bricklaying trade, now predominantly black, white members of a local Washington union were once forbidden from working alongside blacks. In fact, four whites who were found working with blacks on a government job in 1869 were expelled from their union. It was not until sixteen years later that blacks were allowed to form a separate local.[23]

The black population in Washington began to grow during the postwar period, and by 1870 the census showed that over one-third of the population was black. Public works and street work did bring jobs for the day laborers, but gains for local blacks were lessened by the importation of outside labor gangs.[24]

Some technical training for Negroes was made available in 1886 as manual training, carpentry, and metal work were added to the curriculum of "colored" high school education.[25] Public vocational training was not sufficient to overcome years of training deprivation. Moreover, skills learned in schools are quickly lost when not reinforced by experience in the field.

By the end of the century, Washington had the largest Negro urban population in the country, but black mechanics fared much worse than their counterparts in the South.

The black population was expanding rapidly in the latter part of the nineteenth century,[26] but "by 1890, the year of the first federal census of occupations, the proportion of Negroes to all building tradesmen in the South had shrunk to less than one-third."[27] Blacks lost jobs in carpentry and painting but made gains in the trowel trades. During the period from 1890 to 1920, black craftsmen failed to get a proportionate share of the

---

[22] Gunnar Myrdal, *An American Dilemma*, 20th Anniversary Edition, Vol. 1 (New York: McGraw-Hill Book Company, 1964), p. 312.

[23] Spero and Harris, *op. cit.*, p. 18.

[24] Constance McLaughlin Green, *The Secret City, A History of Race Relations in the Nation's Capital* (Princeton: Princeton University Press, 1967) p. 105.

[25] Ingle, *op. cit.*, pp. 31-32.

[26] Green, *op. cit.*, p. 131.

[27] Herbert R. Northrup, *Organized Labor and the Negro* (New York: Kraus Reprint Co., Edition 1971), p. 20.

increased employment opportunities, especially in the electrical, plumbing, and mechanical trades.[28]

By the turn of the century, blacks had adopted a well-established role. As a result of pressure from labor unions, Washington blacks were employed primarily as repairmen and trowel tradesmen in their own community. Furthermore, licensing laws enabled mechanical trade unions to keep blacks out since members of the local were usually on the board of examiners.[29] Thus, in 1900 there were few technically skilled blacks (Table 2).

In Washington, as in the border states, blacks found themselves in a socially and politically southern environment, but one which lacked the advantages of the southern labor market. There was a low percentage of black mechanics, and employers were not accustomed to hiring nonwhites.[30] Some progress was made, however, but mostly in what were to become "Negro crafts." The Bricklayers, for example, amended their constitution to allow the executive board the power to grant a charter to a local if objection to a new local was based on race. Members were subject to a $100

TABLE 2. *Washington Plan*
Negroes in Construction Trades
1900

Trade	Number
Brick and Tile Makers	160
Carpenters and Joiners	235
Cabinet Makers	14
Iron and Steel Workers	25
Marble and Stone Masons and Cutters	337
Painters	149
Plasterers	134
Plumbers and Fitters	85

Source: W.E.B. DuBois, *The Negro American Artisan*, Atlanta University, Series No. 17, 1912 (New York: Arno Press and *The New York Times* Reprint Edition, 1969), p. 45.

---

[28] *Ibid.*, p. 21.

[29] Spero and Harris, *op. cit.*, p. 59.

[30] Northrup, *op. cit.*, p. 22.

fine for discriminating against another member or "blackballing" on other than competency grounds.[31]

THE NEW DEAL TO THE 1960S

The thirties and the Depression brought hardship to Washington blacks although the federal government increased its role in civil rights. Washington private building operations were down by one-third between 1929 and 1930, but this city suffered far less than most. Vast federal building programs supplied jobs for 9,000 men and the District public works added more. Many of the contractors, however, brought in outside labor despite the availability of local workers.[32]

Early signs of the federal government's use of the contract dollar as a lever to increase the number of blacks employed were visible when the WPA Housing Division used a clause in all contracts for cities with large black populations requiring a certain percentage of the payroll to go to blacks. Percentages were based on the 1930 Occupational Census and penalties were set for noncompliance. Although organized labor did much to thwart the plan, some gains were made.[33] In 1934, an advisor on racial matters was appointed in the Department of the Interior and nondiscrimination clauses were added to its contracts. Negroes found manual employment on WPA projects after 1935, partly because of the absence of a color line.[34]

The divorce of the CIO from the AFL brought some hope to organized blacks, because the former espoused a much more progressive stance, especially in the South. The AFL, unfortunately, still controlled the building trades. Not all AFL unions, however, were exclusionary. The hod carriers' and laborers' unions had many blacks. Northrup notes that employers favored blacks in those trades, since "Negroes [were believed] likely to be more amenable to slave-driving." [35]

Union-sponsored laws have assisted organized labor in excluding blacks in the skilled trades. A Maryland law, for example,

---

[31] *Ibid.*, pp. 38-39.

[32] Green, *op. cit.*, p. 219.

[33] Northrup, *op. cit.*, p. 30.

[34] Green, *op. cit.*, p. 231.

[35] Northrup, *op. cit.*, p. 47.

required applicants to have two recommendations from master plumbers, a requirement no black could meet. Despite an end to this law in 1941, licensing and apprenticeship qualifications effectively barred the black man.[36] The electricians, like the plumbers, were highly exclusionary and prompted state and municipal licensing and inspection laws. Less restrictive policies of the international unions were ineffective against local union practices and by the outbreak of World War II blacks faced inferior education and closed doors in all but the trowel trades.

The role of the government in increasing equal employment opportunity expanded during World War II and especially aided black carpenters. When government construction ended, "colored" locals suffered.[37] An interesting forerunner of the Washington Plan, the contract requirements of the U.S. Housing Authority demonstrated the government's interest in pressuring organized labor to employ more blacks in other trades as well. Myrdal points out that contractors had little trouble meeting their "Negro quotas" in unskilled and trowel trades. Many claimed that they were unable to find competent Negroes in the more skilled crafts. Whites opposed such quotas for each craft so vigorously that the USHA had to allow a "blanket" quota for whole projects.[38] There was, however, some truth to the claim that there were few blacks available for skilled work. Years of inferior education and discrimination had taken their toll so that qualifications and skill prerequisites were quite sufficient to keep blacks out.

The war years brought some blacks the construction experience necessary to prove their ability in competition with their white counterparts. Employment was aided by the President's Committee on Fair Employment Practices which had been established in 1941 by President Roosevelt's Executive Order 8802. Discrimination based on race, creed, color, or national origin was prohibited in defense employment or government service.[39] The gains in construction were often limited and many Negroes entered the unions on temporary work permits. Others found only residential or repair work where wages were lower and jobs of

---

[36] *Ibid.*, pp. 24-25.

[37] *Ibid.*, p. 33.

[38] Myrdal, *op. cit.*, pp. 1104-05.

[39] Davie, *op. cit.*, p. 98.

shorter duration. Finally, some D.C. locals continued to resist blacks; their doors would stay closed for years to come.

By the early fifties, through "conferences, persuasion, and prodding, . . . the President's Committee on Government Contracts [PCGC], the Urban League, the NAACP, and other volunteer organizations" made some advances.[40] The PCGC was established by President Eisenhower in 1953 to persuade contractors to practice nondiscrimination in hiring. The PCGC concentrated its work in the manufacturing industry rather than in construction.[41] In 1954, the nondiscrimination clause written into government contracts was strengthened, but black representation in the electro-mechanical unions remained nominal.[42]

As noted earlier, not all unions were exclusionary. The operating engineers' local had over 100 black members, the plasterers' about 40, and the bricklayers' Local 4 was 90 percent black by the end of the 1950s.[43] The Bricklayers' Local 1, on the other hand, was all-white and remains predominantly so even today.

The electrical workers were the most recalcitrant. IBEW Local 26 had a virtual monopoly on electrical labor in Washington. Blacks had to find lower paying work with small nonunion shops, for the doors to Local 26 were closed, and PCGC considered having a GSA contract with a local electrical firm cancelled because of the absence of blacks. By the end of 1958, efforts of the PCGC, President George Meany of the AFL–CIO, the International IBEW Secretary, and the AFL–CIO Civil Rights Committee failed to move Local 26.[44] Meany even offered to recruit nonunion blacks for work on government projects. Local 26 continued to resist and, through its control of the supply of skilled electricians, prevented Meany and civil rights groups from successfully recruiting black electricians.[45] It was not until 1960 that Local 26 allowed one black journeyman to work on a federal site with a permit from the union.

---

[40] Green, *op. cit.*, p. 315.

[41] Ray Marshall, *The Negro Worker* (New York: Random House, 1967), p. 123.

[42] Green, *op. cit.*, p. 314.

[43] *Ibid.*, p. 319.

[44] Ray Marshall, *The Negro and Organized Labor* (New York: John Wiley and Sons, Inc., 1965), p. 114.

[45] *Ibid.*

Efforts by the federal and District governments continued in the early sixties. District Government Organization Order 125 of April 9, 1958, amended May 9, 1961, established the Commissioner's Council on Human Relations in order to secure the adherence of contractors to nondiscrimination clauses in their contracts. Its first chairman, Aaron Goldman, admitted that the Council lacked the power and staff to enforce compliance vigorously.[46]

THE 1960S TO THE PRESENT

President Kennedy established the President's Committee on Equal Employment Opportunity (PCEEO) in May 1961. The PCEEO was granted the power "to publish names of noncomplying contractors and unions, recommend legal action by the Justice Department to prosecute those who failed to comply or furnished false information, cancel the contracts of noncomplying contractors, and prohibit government agencies from entering into new contracts with discriminating employers who had not demonstrated changes in their policies." [47] This committee seemed well equipped to pressure federal contractors into opening their doors to blacks. Many AFL-CIO international unions joined in this spirit by agreeing to provide equal job opportunities, end segregation, eliminate discrimination in apprenticeship, and work with contractors to incorporate nondiscrimination clauses in bargaining agreements.[48] In Washington, as in many other cities, however, the actions of the locals remained the issue.

Table 3 highlights the concentrations of blacks in the building trades since 1900 and shows trends in minority utilization. It should be noted, however, that census data are misleading for two reasons: 1) nonconstruction tradesmen are often included in what would appear to be building skill categories and 2) only field workers (not shop men) are of interest in this study. The reader is also cautioned that these figures are not necessarily representative of minority employment in the union sector. An unknown percentage of the figures comprises the nonunion work force.

---

[46] District of Columbia Advisory Committee to the U.S. Commission on Civil Rights, *Report on Washington, D.C.: Employment*, 1963, p. 35.

[47] Marshall, *The Negro Worker, op. cit.*, pp. 124-125.

[48] *Ibid.*, p. 125.

TABLE 3. Washington Plan
Male Construction Employment by Race, District of Columbia
1900-1960

Occupation	1900			1910			1920			1930		
	Total	Black	Percent Black	Total	Black	Percent Black	Total	Black	Percent Black	Total	Black	Percent Black
Carpenters	2,298	236	10.3	2,769	286	10.3	3,014	217	7.2	3,298	315	9.6
Electricians	461 a	12 a	2.6	968 a	22 a	2.3	1,422	30	2.1	1,564	67	4.3
Masons, Tilesetters, and Stone Cutters	1,425	337	23.6	968	138	14.3	757	103	13.6	1,348	243	18.0
Painters, Paperhangers, nad Glaziers	1,804	172	9.5	1,773	211	11.9	1,680	162	9.6	2,896	390	13.5
Plasterers and Cement Finishers	465	134	28.8	603	192	31.8	476	184	38.7	894	409	45.7
Plumbers & Pipefitters	1,074	85	7.9	1,286	74	5.8	1,360	45	3.3	1,590	100	6.3
Structural Metalworkers	300	25	8.3	NA	NA	—	NA	NA	—	227	2	0.9
Laborers & Helpers	NA	NA	—	744	631	84.8	3,799	3,284	86.4	4,451	3,768	84.7
Roofers b	NA	NA	—	396	31	7.8	471	34	7.2	540	26	4.8

	1940			1950			1960		
Carpenters	2,723	236	8.7	2,739	374	13.7	1,397	474	33.9
Electricians	1,479	51	3.4	1,645	134	8.1	397	186	25.2
Masons, Tilesetters, and Stone Cutters	1,467	272	18.5	1,901	766	40.3	1,118	713	63.8
Painters, Paperhangers, and Glaziers	2,925	398	13.6	2,866	596	20.8	2,182	933	42.8
Plasterers and Cement Finishers	753	348	46.2	1,179	754	64.0	885	728	82.3
Plmbers & Pipefitters	1,457	86	5.9	1,672	182	10.9	871	214	24.6
Structural Metalworkers	332	8	2.4	293	8	2.7	102	12	11.8
Laborers & Helpers	6,317	5,076	80.4	7,703	6,872	89.2	5,863	5,433	92.7
Roofers	691	54	7.8	618	24	3.9	290	62	21.4

Source: *U.S. Census of Population:*

1900: Special Reports, *Occupations, States and Territories,* Table 41.
1910: Vol. IV, *Occupation Statistics,* Table VII.
1920: Vol. IV, *Occupations,* Chap. VII, Table 1.
1930: Vol. IV, *Occupations by States,* Table 11.
1940: Vol. III, *The Labor Force,* Part 2, Table 13.
1950: Vol. II, *Characteristics of the Population,* Part 9, Table 77.
1960: Vol. I, *Characteristics of the Population,* Part 10, Table 122.

a Includes electrical engineers.
b Includes tinsmiths, coppersmiths, and some sheet metal workers.

The percentages of blacks found in the trades shown in Table 3 may seem higher than expected. It should be noted, however, that the proportion of blacks in the indicated skill categories represents center city workers only. Construction unions have jurisdictions which cover the metropolitan area and, in some cases, larger areas of Virginia and Maryland. Thus, the percentages of blacks represented in construction as union members were much smaller than the percentages in Table 3. As is true today, federal construction work offered the most lucrative contracts and steady employment. Blacks, left to nonunion residential and private work, were lower paid and removed from the skill-improving heavy construction. White unionists maintained command of the federal construction dollar.

In the mid–sixties, while enforcement of nondiscrimination was scattered throughout the District government, the federal government was making moves to end discrimination. In addition to the Civil Rights Act of 1964, the federal government focused particular attention on apprenticeship. In June 1963, the Apprenticeship Information Center (AIC) for the District of Columbia was opened with the help of the Labor Department and the support of organized labor. Although establishing the AIC scarcely removed the "secrecy and silence about what goes on in apprenticeship training" as Boris Shishkin, Director of the Civil Rights Department of the AFL-CIO, implied it would, this municipal agency helped close the gap between the local labor supply and apprenticeship programs.[49] Prior to 1963, the government's role in apprenticeship consisted primarily of the D.C. Apprenticeship Council. The Council was criticized for failing to coordinate apprenticeship activities effectively among the schools, other government agencies, and the joint apprenticeship committees.[50]

Added pressure resulted from the adoption of new selection standards by the Bureau of Apprenticeship and Training (BAT). Despite labor's opposition, apprentice selection procedures were to be based on objective standards and equal opportunity. Weak penalites were provided for noncomplying programs.[51] As in its municipal counterpart, organized labor was well represented in the Bureau and little enforcement resulted.

---

[49] Testimony of Boris Shishkin, as cited in District of Columbia Advisory Committee, *op. cit.*, p. 22.

[50] *Ibid.*, p. 42.

[51] Marshall, *The Negro Worker*, *op. cit.*, p. 126.

Title VII of the Civil Rights Act of 1964 gave the government the legal means to end discrimination regardless of whether or not the employer was a federal contractor. Unions were specifically affected by Section 703(c), which prohibits discrimination in referrals, and Section 703(d) which forbids any employer, union, or joint labor-management committee which controls apprenticeship or other training programs from discriminating.[52] The question arose, however, whether equal treatment would provide equal opportunity, for blacks have lacked the education and other advantages enjoyed by whites. Even if not racially motivated, organized labor could often reduce the number of outside entrants by concensus of the voting membership, use of examinations, licensing, and nepotism.

Although laws and regulations might not have been strictly enforced, liberalized attitudes and the threat of enforcement combined to win more jobs for blacks. Negroes entering construction apprenticeships increased from 61 in 1963, 99 in 1964, 156 in 1965, 256 in 1967, to 349 in 1968.[53] As in the past, progress depended on the trade. By the end of 1965, seven unions had no blacks in apprenticeship: Sheet Metal Workers, Asbestos Workers, Glaziers, Painters, Lathers, Stone and Marble Masons, and the Tile and Terrazzo Workers.[54] In 1967, a survey by the D.C. Commissioner's Council on Human Relations revealed that in a city that was then 65 percent black, only 18.9 percent of the employees in construction were black. More important, 65.2 percent of the laborers were black but only 10.4 percent of the skilled craftsmen were black.

Organized labor was the center of controversy during many of the civil rights struggles of the late sixties. White work crews doing urban renewal construction in the central sections of cities like Washington were highly visible irritants to the black community. When such renewal resulted in the construction of middle and upper income housing primarily for white occupancy, tempers raged.[55]

---

[52] *Ibid.*, p. 134.

[53] Ray Marshall and Vernon M. Briggs, Jr., *The Negro and Apprenticeship* (Baltimore: The Johns Hopkins Press, 1967), pp. 154-155.

[54] *Ibid.*, p. 153.

[55] George Strauss and Sidney Ingerman, "Public Policy and Discrimination in Apprenticeship," in *Negroes and Jobs*, Louis A. Ferman, *et al.*, eds. (Ann Arbor: University of Michigan Press, 1968), pp. 314-315.

As doors were opened to blacks, the apprenticeship route of entry evolved into "the way" for blacks to get into the union. Blacks faced tests and interviews, as well as hours of evening classes, while knowing that the majority of building tradesmen had not completed apprenticeship. *The 1964 Manpower Report of the President* indicated that only 39.4 percent of construction craftsmen learned their trade through formal training with a low of 11.2 percent for some employed as operating engineers and a high of 72.9 percent for electricians.[56] Unions, however, point out that as building skills grow more technical, apprenticeship will become almost mandatory for all new entrants, white or black.

In all fairness, it must be said that discrimination in the building trades is not totally racial. Craft unionists are intensely loyal to their trade and unions. The Washington unions knew that opening their ranks to many new entrants, regardless of race, would diminish their control of the labor supply. The desire for such control is largely economically motivated.

The decade of the 1960s has seen progress to end discrimination on many fronts. Pressure from blacks and civil rights groups; the increased use of blacks during labor shortages; open-shop competition; the unions' need for black support for political objectives; legal action by the EEOC, the Department of Justice, and the courts; District government action; the NLRB; and progressive efforts by organized labor have all contributed toward a moderation of attitudes concerning blacks in employment.[57]

The 1960s saw the rapid growth of the suburbs and a boom in federal and private construction. The Bureau of Labor Statistics found that during the period from 1960-1969 contract construction employment had risen over one-third in the Standard Metropolitan Statistical Area (SMSA), but had dropped by one-eighth in the District.[58] Much of the new work went to white craftsmen from Maryland and Virginia. Construction wage rates grew at a phenomenal rate to a point where the crafts offered entrance into the middle-income class and a way out of the ghetto. By 1969, construction again become the center of controversy as black groups and civil rights organizations concentrated their efforts on union-dominated federal contract construction.

---

[56] U.S. Department of Labor, *Manpower Report of the President* (Washington: United States Government Printing Office, 1964), p. 257.

[57] Marshall, *The Negro Worker, op. cit.*, pp. 150-151.

[58] Testimony at Washington Plan Hearings, April 1970.

SUMMARY

This brief history is intended to show the roots of the current controversy surrounding the Washington Plan. Events of the past few years cannot be viewed in a vacuum, for many of the arguments, frustrations, and charges have been voiced in the past. By searching the history of blacks in construction, one can better understand the problems the federal government must face in its latest attempt to bring about truly equal employment opportunity in this industry.

This background has omitted a discussion of Executive Order 11246 and the advent of the Philadelphia Plan. Furthermore, local events such as the forming of the Washington Area Construction Industry Task Force and the Mayor's Committee on Construction, the establishment of Project BUILD, the beginnings of METRO, and the other efforts by industry, labor, community, and government have not been covered. These events, however, are an integral part of the beginnings of the first federally imposed hiring plan in Washington. Our field study report which follows will treat each as it affects the Washington Plan.

CHAPTER IV

The Evolution of the Washington Plan

The establishment of the Philadelphia Plan in 1969 signaled a new period of government regulation of the construction industry. In the spirit of Executive Order 11246, the Department of Labor instituted an affirmative action program for construction contractors who employed individuals in trades that showed a history of underutilization of minorities. With promises to meet the percentage goals specified by the Plan written into federal contracts, contractors were thus obligated to increase the employment of minorities, or show a "good faith" effort to meet those goals. Philadelphia became one of the first cities in the country to be included in a now growing list of imposed and voluntary hiring plans in construction.

A construction hiring plan for Washington was inevitable. In no other city does the federal government possess greater financial leverage over construction contractors. Almost all of the lucrative, heavy construction is either directly or indirectly financed by the government.

Government action appeared even more necessary because minorities were almost nonexistent in many of the skilled construction crafts, despite their overwhelming majority in the city's population. Approximately 71 percent of the District's population is nonwhite. In addition, Washington's status as the nation's capital demanded action.

Although government, industry, labor, and community leaders had pressed for greater minority involvement in construction, it was not until the late 1960s that the federal government contemplated a comprehensive plan to use the federal dollar to achieve this socioeconomic objective. The impetus for such a plan came from the Department of Labor, but militant action by community leaders made the advent of the Washington Plan a controversial and well-publicized event.

COMMUNITY ROLE AND OFFICIAL ACTION

In the fall of 1969, the Washington Urban League formed a special task force to address the problem of exclusionary practices in the construction industry. The Washington Area Construction Industry Task Force (WACITF) was established and became a loose coalition of community organizations as listed in Table 4.

Many community and civil rights organizations, including those shown in Table 4, demanded additional jobs for minori-

TABLE 4. *Washington Plan*
*Participating Organizations in the Washington
Area Construction Industry Task Force*

Washington Urban League
NAACP
Pride, Inc.
Model Inner City Community Organization
Community Planning
Peoples Involvement Corporation
Unity House
Washington Area Black American Law Students
OIC
Electrical Contractors and Masters Apprenticeship Company, Inc.
National Urban Coalition
Central City Community Corporation

Organizations supporting their effort were:
Black United Front
UPO—Manpower Division
Capitol East Community Organization
Center for Community Change
CHANGE, Inc.
Archdiocesan Urban Affairs Office
Council of Churches
Concerned Citizens for Central Cardoza
Jewish Community Council
American Friends Service Committee
American Jewish Congress
CHASE, Inc.
National Council of Negro Women, Inc.
Uptown Progress
Human Relations Commission
Friendship House
Columbia Heights Community Association
American Jewish Committee

ties in construction and progressive contractors and their associations were formulating affirmative action programs. By 1969, organized labor had a well-established training program, Project BUILD, to complement "outreach" programs and other efforts to increase the number of minorities in apprenticeship. Various agencies of the district government were also pushing for change. Thus, 1969 saw increased awareness of the complaints of the minority community and some concrete progress.

However, minorities were finding neither long-term opportunities nor dramatically increased membership in construction unions. In November 1969, the WACITF decided to bring public attention to this issue by focusing on the construction of the new subway system, METRO. Although community efforts in the past had brought attention to exclusion in the industry in general, WACITF chose METRO because of the massive size of the project, the involvement of federal money, and the fact that the subway would be built in the city to serve the community. METRO became the target for community demands for increased employment and financial participation by minorities in construction.

In response to inquiries made by WACITF, the Office of Federal Contract Compliance (OFCC) designated the Department of Transportation (DOT) as the agency responsible for contracts let by the Washington Metropolitan Area Transit Authority (WMATA) within the meaning of Executive Order 11246. On February 3, 1970, the OFCC directed DOT to develop an affirmative action program with WMATA and all contractors and subcontractors working on METRO construction.

On March 2, 1970, the OFCC indicated its intention to use goals and timetables similar to those found in the Philadelphia Plan. John Wilks, then Director of OFCC, instructed DOT to "include specific ranges for the employment of minorities, even if this necessitates a delay in awarding the contracts." [59] On that same day, Department of Transportation secretary John Volpe suspended the awarding of construction contracts pending the development of an adequate affirmative action program. During this time, the WACITF continued to attack aggressively federal contracting procedures.

The first step in the development of a minority hiring plan for all federal construction in the District was taken on April

---

[59] Letter from John Wilks to Richard F. Lally, Director of Civil Rights, Department of Transportation, March 2, 1970.

2, 1970, when it was announced that the Department of Labor would hold hearings on April 13 and 14 to gather information on minority utilization in the Washington, D.C. construction industry.

Notice of the hearing announced that "data, views, or arguments [were] to be considered by the Office of Federal Contract Compliance in implementing the requirements and objectives of Executive Order 11246 in federally-involved construction in the Washington, D.C. area."

The specific information requested was to include, but not be limited to, the following:

1. the current extent of minority group participation in each construction trade, and the full employee complement of each trade;

2. a statement and evaluation of present employee recruitment methods, as well as the assistance and effectiveness of any employer or union programs to increase minority participation in the trades;

3. the availability of qualified and qualifiable minority group persons for employment in each construction trade, including where they are now working, how they may be brought into the trades, etc.;

4. an evaluation of existing training programs in the area, including the number of minorities and others recruited into the programs, the number who complete training, the length and extent of training, employer experience with trainees, the need for additional or expanded training programs, etc.;

5. an analysis of the number of additional workers that could be absorbed into each trade without displacing present employees, including consideration of present employee shortages, projected growth of the trade, projected employee turnover, etc.;

6. the availability and utilization of minority contractors on federally-involved contracts; and

7. the desirability and extent, including the geographical scope, of possible federal action to ensure equal employment opportunity in the construction trades.[60]

Written responses were invited and those desiring to reply orally were offered the opportunity to address a panel to be convened by the OFCC.

---

[60] Office of Federal Contract Compliance, Notice of Hearing, April 2, 1970.

The notice also stated that it was

> the declared policy of the Department of Labor that a local agreement among contractors, unions and minority groups in the community is preferable to the imposition of specific requirements by this Department. Thus, if such an agreement can be reached for the Washington, D.C. area prior to June 1, 1970, the Department will not need to impose Federal requirements. However, if an agreement is not concluded by that date, this Department will immediately proceed to implement its responsibilities consistent with the information it obtains from the hearings herein noticed and from other sources.

Notices were mailed to "over 400 contractors, labor officials, community organizations, Federal agencies and persons known to be interested in equal employment opportunity in the Washington area." [61]

The announcement brought a varied response. Some members of the community saw an opportunity to voice their complaints of exclusion from segments of the industry. Industry representatives prepared descriptions of their own progressive plans to upgrade minorities. Some labor officials perceived a parallel to the recent Philadelphia Plan case and reacted adversely to the prospect of increased government intervention. Although many representatives from labor and industry accepted the invitation to testify, others refused to participate in any way. The threat of an imposed plan was either not taken seriously or deemed inevitable. A frequent reason for apprehension and subsequent refusal to attend was the fear that industry or labor leaders would have to present racial statistics which would be damaging. Absence could do no more harm, some believed.

The prospect of a Washington Plan certainly affected events surrounding the now controversial METRO subway system. On March 17, a DOT decision to proceed with METRO contracts, pending the development of a Washington Plan, evoked strong opposition from community representatives who wanted concrete hiring plans written into all METRO contracts. With assurances that action would be taken by the Department of Labor (DOL), Secretary of Transportation Volpe, on April 8, 1970, had WMATA postpone bid openings until a plan was established. Only days later, the Secretary included all DOT funded or assisted projects in the Washington Standard Metropolitan

[61] U.S. Department of Labor, News Release, USDL-11-152, Thursday, April 9, 1970.

Statistical Area (SMSA)[62] in this bid freeze. Secretary Volpe wrote, "I intend that DOT will cooperate in the development, implementation and enforcement of the Washington Plan. Here in the Nation's capital, we must set the example for others, especially in the matter of providing and assuring opportunity and affirmative action."[63]

The Hearings

The hearings began amidst controversy on April 13 and fell far short of the aims articulated by Director Wilks when the purpose of the hearings was announced. Representatives of the WACITF condemned the lack of cross-examination of witnesses. Former Assistant Secretary of Labor Arthur A. Fletcher, who conducted the hearings, denied this request for cross-examination because he felt that the hearings would be prolonged.

Assistant Secretary Fletcher also warned that a government plan, prepared by the Labor Department, would go into effect on June 1, as promised, if a voluntary solution was not reached. Such a plan, he indicated, would include goals for the percentages of minorities employed in each specified craft.

The hearings were well publicized and individual testimony brought a great deal of attention to the problem of minority exclusion from the skilled construction trades. Most of the attention fell on the union sector of the industry. In fact, little was presented to establish the intent or nature of the nonunion sector's record of minority utilization.

Many unions sent no representative; others demonstrated varying degrees of cooperation. Some presented racial statistics, while others presented only estimates. It is unclear if or how such data were verified. Governmental officials and community representatives compiled data on union membership by citing surveys, but estimates were varied and the data often quite old. One union cited membership statistics as a demonstration of good faith and the panel appeared to respond favorably to this show of good will. The data, however, in fact the precise figures, are still used almost two years later to indicate the extent

---

[62] Washington SMSA: District of Columbia; Montgomery, Prince Georges, Arlington, Fairfax, Loudoun, and Prince Williams Counties; Alexandria, Fairfax, and Falls Church.

[63] Memorandum to Heads of Operating Administrations, Department of Transportation, from the Secretary, April 10, 1970.

of minority membership in the union. Ironically, the corroborating sources available to those who would check the veracity of these figures contain the same information, voluntarily given by the union itself.

Some testimony aroused militant community representatives. For example, one federal agency reported that out of twenty-eight contractors receiving federal funds in the metropolitan area, nineteen were admittedly not in compliance with Executive Order 11246. As a result, members of WACITF challenged the government's willingness to pursue vigorously equal employment opportunity. Mistrust of compliance enforcement was deepened by the knowledge that no federal contractor had thus far been debarred from federal contracts.

In addition, many representatives from the government, community, labor, and industry described upgrading efforts in other areas and offered suggestions for the development of a new equal employment program. Representatives of apprentice "outreach" programs, minority construction firms, vocational schools, citizens' groups, contractors' associations, and unions described current recruiting and training programs. Others addressed the problem of finding the number of minority applicants required to meet a new affirmative action program. Many representatives from labor and the industry contended that few minorities have sought construction employment even when it has been available. Community spokesmen firmly denied that anything less than discrimination is the cause for low minority representation in the skilled trades.

Throughout the hearings, WACITF grew more militant and critical of the proceedings. Task Force members were even assisted by a caucus of black congressional leaders who publicly supported their views. Spokesmen called for the use of "manning tables" rather than Philadelphia-type plans. Manning tables, they argued, would list the number of minorities to be hired in each craft and be incorporated into each contract. The strength of such a plan would be in the binding nature of the contract, whereas a plan requiring good faith effort is harder to enforce.

The hearings ended with no clear indication that a voluntary solution was possible. Although WACITF appeared to be a strong voice in the community, no true spokesman for black workers was identified. Despite their majority status in Washington, blacks were not organized.

Spokesmen from the industry and labor testified that some progress had been and continued to be made in hiring and upgrading blacks, but the sparse data presented could not establish that any breakthrough was in progress. The absence of information from several important areas of the industry and organized labor, because of lack of interest or refusal to testify, forced Department of Labor officials to rely on secondary sources when determining their policy.

Negotiations and Plan Imposition

After the hearings, the Department of Labor asked representatives of the community, industry, and labor to develop a "hometown" plan by June 1, 1970.

Private meetings began shortly after the hearings. Department of Labor officials offered assistance and samples of existing affirmative action plans. The community position was to be presented by the WACITF. Several contractor association representatives and area labor leaders were also available to voice industry and union views. Although many of the participants were recognized leaders in their sector, some segments were underrepresented and no spokesman from the nonunion sector was involved.

Cooperation seemed unlikely from the outset. Procedures for the negotiations were agreed upon with difficulty, thus leaving matters of substance essentially untouched. A moderator, the Reverend David H. Eaton, then Chairman of the D.C. Human Relations Commission, was wisely selected. Reverend Eaton won the respect of industry and labor negotiators, yet remained sensitive to community needs.

Actual negotiations did not begin until only days before the June 1 deadline. The Task Force, however, demanded that 70 to 80 percent of all construction work in each craft be done by minorities. Although little was offered by organized labor, compromise seemed impossible as long as those demands remained non-negotiable. By May 29, the Task Force made it clear that no negotiations would occur before the Department of Labor issued its minority hiring plan. Representatives of the Task Force stuck to their demand that the racial makeup of each craft reflect the majority status of blacks in the District, then 71 percent. They felt that an area-wide set of goals would be unrealistic in that the suburbs were overwhelmingly white.

Inner city blacks, they believed, should do most of the rebuilding of the community and not work in outlying Virginia and Maryland suburbs.

Not unexpectedly, negotiations broke down. Industry spokesmen adopted a "go slow" position, according to the community representatives, while WACITF continued to demand a 70 to 80 percent minority representation. As a result, an adversary relationship, rather than cooperative negotiations, developed. The community representatives had a mistrust of voluntarism and were wary of a labor-industry alliance that would provide some marginal progress, but no real breakthrough.

On June 1, 1970, the Department of Labor issued the Washington Plan and spokesmen from each segment of the controversy were swift to criticize it. Ironically, members of WACITF and the unions were in agreement, but for different reasons. The contractors, who would bear the brunt of the Plan's requirements, were much less vocal, but nonetheless aware of the problems they would soon face. WACITF immediately condemned the Plan's goal of increasing minority participation in the trades to match the proportion of minorities in the SMSA (roughly 26 percent), not the District alone. Task Force spokesmen pointed out that

> it serves little purpose to offer an unemployed but eligible black construction worker residing in D.C. a job in Reston, Virginia or some other remote construction site when in his own city the overwhelming majority of jobs will continue to go to whites. Washington residents fully deserve an opportunity to build their own city; the Department of Labor Plan clearly denies them this right.[64]

Furthermore, the maximum increase required for all the eleven crafts specifically designated by the Washington Plan was only 43 percent, far below the population proportion of the city.

WACITF voiced other criticisms, as follows: several major crafts, such as the carpenters, operating engineers, rodmen, and plasterers were excluded from coverage; low goals were set for the sheet metal workers, an historically exclusionary union; existing federal contracts would not be covered by the Plan; good faith requirements were vague, thus providing a loophole; the plan would not cover contracts whose bids were solicited before June 1 (which included some METRO contracts); the problems of minority contractors were not addressed; and the promise of only the 3,500 jobs noted in the Plan would hardly

---

[64] *Construction Labor Report*, No. 768, June 10, 1970, p. A-18.

constitute a success if there were as many minority workers available for construction work as the Department of Labor estimates. Opportunity for community review and adequate on-the-job training (OJT) provisions were also found lacking.

In general, however, the community recognized that the imposition of the Washington Plan was an historic event. The government appeared willing to confront industry and union interests in an attempt to accelerate the return of the black worker to the construction crafts. Skeptics were determined to watch the government's actions closely, however, as the Task Force and other groups affirmed their intention to continue pressure on the Department of Labor and to establish a monitoring system to ensure vigorous enforcement of the Plan by the government.

Nonpublic reaction covered a wide spectrum of views. Reaction from the construction industry was reserved. Many contractors were frustrated because the Plan had curtailed their hopes of working out a self-policed plan, as some contractors' associations had already developed their own affirmative action plans. One representative, the Executive Secretary of the Construction Contractors Council, said that meeting the goals "is going to be a problem but I think we'll be able to surmount it." [65] A few contractors appeared determined to resist the government's intrusion into the competitive system—"anti-American," some said. Others saw in the plan an opportunity to regain the control of hiring that had been lost to the unions. Nonfederal and most nonunion contractors practically ignored the controversy surrounding the Plan.

Criticism from organized labor was strong. The Executive Secretary of the Washington Building and Construction Trades Council called the Plan's percentage goals unattainable and based on erroneous data. A spokesman said that "even if all . . . the trades . . . take in minority applicants for the next four years, they cannot reach the percentages stipulated by the Department of Labor." [66] Most labor leaders emphasized that Washington labor unions had a record far better than their counterparts in other cities and that several training programs such as Project BUILD were moving to bring more blacks into the construction trades.

---

[65] *Washington Post*, June 4, 1970.

[66] *Ibid.*

The range of union attitudes was as varied as that of their industry counterparts. Several unions, which had remained aloof from the hearings and pre-imposition negotiations, retained a wait-and-see attitude, determined not to act without direct pressure from the government. Other labor leaders, such as the spokesman of the Building Trades Council, expressed dissatisfaction, but no intention to resist. "Most certainly we'll comply to the best of our ability," he said, "if we can get the people. We must comply." [67]

In the weeks that followed, the Department of Labor strived to accomplish the tremendous task of creating a compliance mechanism, informing affected parties of their responsibilities under the Plan, and developing a reporting system to accumulate the data necessary to monitor the effectiveness of the Plan.

THE WASHINGTON PLAN

The Washington Plan affirmative action program to assure compliance with equal employment opportunity requirements of Executive Order 11246 for federally involved construction contractors was issued on June 1, 1970 and was published in the Federal Register. The Plan became Part 60-5, Title 41 of the Code of Federal Regulations; Chapter 60 applying to the Office of Federal Contract Compliance, Equal Employment Opportunity, Department of Labor.[68]

The purpose of the Plan is "to implement the provisions of Executive Order 11246 . . . requiring a program of equal employment opportunity by Federal contractors and subcontractors and Federally-assisted construction contractors and subcontractors in the Washington Standard Metropolitan Statistical Area (SMSA)." [69] All contractors with a project in excess of $500,000 are covered by the Plan unless the OFCC accepts an area-wide agreement for the trade involved or unless the trade is part of a multi-trade agreement among contractors, unions, and the community. Acceptance of these alternatives, however, is subject to the discretion of the OFCC. For those projects covered,

---

[67] *Ibid.*

[68] The authority for the Plan is found in Sections 201, 202, 205, 211, 301, 302, and 303 of E.O. 11246, 30 FR 12319, and Sections 60-1.1 and 60-1.40, Title 41, Code of Federal Regulations.

[69] CFR, Title 41, Part 60-5.1, Subpart A. Provisions of Part 60-5 appear at 35 FR 19352.

contractors and subcontractors must agree to meet sepecified goal ranges for the employment of minorities in eleven designated trades. An outline of the requirements of the Washington Plan is presented below.

The Washington Plan includes an evaluation of the status of minorities in the construction trades. The percentage of minorities in Washington unions was used to support the conclusion that minorities were seriously underrepresented in many skilled trades.

It is unclear to the reader of the Plan, however, how the data in Table 5 were compiled. The April hearings were noted as a source, but it is believed that the table was derived from a variety of sources not cited.

Based on such findings, those trades with a high percentage of minority workers were excluded from the Plan's coverage.

TABLE 5. *Washington Plan*
Percentage Minority Representation in D.C. Building Trades

Union	Percent Minority
Asbestos Workers	1.4
Boilermakers	0.0
Bricklayers	56.9
Carpenters	16.2
Cement Masons	71.1
Electricians	4.8
Elevator Constructors	10.6
Glaziers	3.3
Iron Workers	3.2
Laborers	90.6
Lathers	10.0
Operating Engineers	24.4
Pipefitters-Plumbers-Steamfitters	4.1
Plasterers	25.4
Reinforcing Rodmen	32.4
Roofers	85.3
Sheet Metal Workers	1.1
Teamsters	87.0
Tile and Terrazzo Workers	3.6
Painters and Paperhangers	6.6

Source: CFR, Title 41, Part 60-5-11 (b), Statistical Data.

In addition, the carpenters, rodmen, plasterers, and operating engineers were specifically excluded. Apparently there was a cut-off percentage, below which trades would be included. We question the exclusion of the carpenters, however, in that, according to the figures noted in Table 5, that trade possesses a minority proportion below the population proportion for the SMSA. If the latter proportion, 26 percent, represents an overall target for minority representation in the construction trades, it would seem likely that the Plan would encourage the carpenters to improve their record. Testimony by the carpenters' representative, on the other hand, may have indicated that upgrading efforts in progress would achieve such a representative proportion by 1974, the final year of the Washington Plan.

The anticipated sources of new minority craftsmen were discussed in the Plan. As many as 73,000 minorities were estimated to be unemployed in the SMSA and approximately 15,000 minority laborers were felt to be candidates for movement into more skilled trades. Vocational schools; graduates of MDTA, OIC, and other training programs; employment services; Project BUILD; and community organizations were but a few sources of minority applicants. In sum, the Plan estimated that "45,000 to 60,000 minority workers presently [are] available for construction employment and/or training, and recruitable through concerted efforts by contractors, unions and, particularly, minority community groups." [70] It was held that the use of minority contractors as subcontractors on federal construction projects would also increase the employment of minorities. Finally, the Plan promised government support of the training necessary to give many of the minorities the skills required for skilled construction work.

The goals and timetables, which become the heart of government-imposed plans, were developed from estimates of death, retirement, disability, and out-migration in each craft. Figures for percentages of annual new openings were presented for electricians, painters and paperhangers, plumbers, pipefitters and steamfitters, iron workers, and sheet metal workers. Then, in the absence of estimates for the elevator constructors, asbestos workers, lathers, boilermakers, tile and terrazzo workers, and glaziers, an average of the annual rate of the previous five trades, 12.4 percent, was to be used. The lack of availability of a better

---

[70] CFR, Title 41, Paragraph 60-5.12(e).

method is unquestioned, but the use of such an imprecise measure has certainly attracted much criticism.

The Washington Plan designates the following eleven trades to be covered:

Asbestos Workers
Boilermakers
Electricians
Elevator Constructors
Glaziers
Iron Workers
Lathers
Painters and Paperhangers
Pipefitters-Plumbers-Steamfitters
Sheet Metal Workers
Tile and Terrazzo Workers

No trade is required to exclude white applicants, but hiring one black for every two openings is advised. Using such a program, the Plan estimates approximately 3,500 minorities should be added to the industry in the above trades by the end of the Plan. The purpose of establishing ranges for each trade is that "by establishing ranges which anticipate good faith efforts by construction contractors to fill new and vacated jobs on at least a 1-to-1 minority-to-nonminority basis through May 1974, contractors should be able to meet their commitments through effective affirmative recruitment efforts from available minority manpower without displacing any existing craftsmen and without discriminating against any nonminority applicant for employment." [71]

Requirements of the Washington Plan

All bidders for federal or federally assisted contracts or subcontracts whose estimated cost exceeds $500,000 must submit, prior to the bid opening, a document which outlines the specific goals of minority utilization in each of the eleven trades covered by the Plan during the life of the contract for all work done within the Washington SMSA. The goals must be within the ranges specified by the Plan for trades employed by the contractor in performance of the federally involved contract. No negotiation of these goals is permitted after the opening of bids

---

[71] CFR, Title 41, Paragraph 60-5.15(d).

and prior to the awarding of the contract. Contracting agencies, such as HEW, GSA, and DOD, must require that all contractors agree to achieve at least the minimums for the ranges given in Table 6.

The goals set for each participating contractor or subcontractor will cover all work, federal and private, and the man-hours of minority employment must be substantially uniform throughout the contract. Thus, the Plan is intended to ensure long-term employment throughout the life of the contract, not sporadic hirings for the purpose of achieving yearly deadlines.

Each contractor is given three opportunities for compliance:

1. by achieving the required minority utilization rates throughout his work in the SMSA (federal and nonfederal);

2. by proving that he is a member of a contractor association which is expanding the employment of minorities and reflects an association-wide utilization rate of all member sites in the SMSA which meets the goals of the Plan; or

TABLE 6. *Washington Plan*
Percentage Minority Utilization Ranges Under
Washington Plan

Trade	Percentage Range of Minority Employment Until:			
	May 31, 1971	May 31, 1972	May 31, 1973	May 31, 1974
Electricians	10-16	16-22	22-28	28-34
Painters and Paperhangers	14-21	21-28	28-35	35-42
Plumbers, Pipefitters & Steamfitters	10-15	15-20	20-25	25-30
Iron Workers	11-19	19-27	27-35	35-43
Sheet Metal Workers	7-13	13-19	19-25	25-31
Elevator Constructors	16-22	22-28	28-34	34-40
Asbestos Workers	8-14	14-20	20-26	26-32
Lathers	16-22	22-28	28-34	34-40
Boiler Makers	6-12	12-18	18-24	24-30
Tile and Terrazzo Workers	10-16	16-22	22-28	28-34
Glaziers	10-16	16-22	22-28	28-34

Source: CFR, Title 41, Part 60.5.

3. by utilizing a union or organization that supplies over 80 percent of his manpower needs and demonstrates a minority utilization rate for the craft involved that meets the contractor's Plan commitments.

No contractor, on the other hand, would be in compliance if he has actually denied equal employment opportunity.

In sum, the contractor must meet the goals noted above throughout his work force unless his contractor association or referral union possesses the requisite proportion of minorities in the covered trades. The last two alternatives are not likely to be utilized.

Contractors unable to meet the specific goals may still be in compliance if found to have made a "good faith effort" to meet the goals. The Washington Plan includes an outline of various actions by the contractor which would constitute good faith. Increased communication with community groups, maintenance of records on minority applicants, efforts to provide training, notification to OFCC when unions interfere with the achievement of a contractor's goals, disseminating an equal employment policy, special recruiting efforts, encouraging minority employees to seek others, and utilizing minority subcontractors are some of the recommendations.

Contracting agencies are instructed to review contractors' employment practices during the period of the contracts. Failure to meet the goals set forth in a contract will result in the contractor's having to prove his good faith effort to the agency involved. That their referral unions have not supplied the requested minority workers is no excuse, because the responsibility for meeting the goals remains solely with the contractor or subcontractor.

Each prime contractor is required to include his commitment to meet Washington Plan goals in each subcontract for work in any of the specified trades. Thus, the subcontractor is held accountable for meeting the goal commitments no matter how small the size of the subcontract. The prime contractor is not accountable for the noncompliance of a subcontractor, although he is still required to report failure to fulfill contract obligations to OFCC and the contracting agency. This point is crucial in that the designated skilled trades are most often employed by small, special contractors who do subcontracting work for large federal contractors.

Two mechanisms for review of the Plan are also provided. Paragraph 60-5.15(e) states that the "Department shall make every effort to encourage and develop a voluntary committee representing these three groups (contractors, labor, and community), which committee shall periodically review the effectiveness of this Order and make advisory recommendations to the Department regarding this Order." The establishment of the Washington Plan Review Committee, chaired by the Director of OFCC, meets that provision. Furthermore, the Plan provides for a review of the standards (trades and ranges) in order to determine "whether the projections on which these standards are based adequately reflect the construction labor market situation at that time." [72]

Other provisions enable agency heads to exempt a contract on the grounds of national security interests. Special requests for exemptions by contractors must be made and justified in writing to the Director of OFCC.

Like its counterpart in Philadelphia, the Washington Plan poses a real threat to the noncomplying contractor. If found not in compliance, a contractor may be debarred from any further government work. Such a ruling could force many large construction firms out of business. Although the debarment threat once appeared hollow to many community critics, several debarments have in fact occurred in Philadelphia, and the courts have upheld the federal government's right to require acceptance of the Philadelphia Plan stipulations as a prerequisite for receiving a construction contract. [73]

---

[72] CFR, Title 41, Paragraph 60-5.21(c)(1).

[73] *Contractors' Association of Eastern Pennsylvania* v. *Shultz*, 311 F. Supp. 1002 (E.D. Pa., 1970); affirmed 442 F.2d 159 (3rd cir., 1971); cert. denied, 404 U.S. 854 (1971).

CHAPTER V

Washington Plan Data Analysis

One drawback of an imposed plan is the lack of a centralized administering body from which hiring data may be received. In order to make a comprehensive evaluation of any affirmative action program, the progress of each employer in carrying out the requirements of the plan must be examined. Furthermore, full assessment of the performance of each craft can be made only if data are available which reveal all the new entries and exits by race during the period under evaluation. Unfortunately, no one source of these data exists for the Washington Plan.

Given this constraint, we have attempted to develop an accurate evaluation of the Washington Plan by employing alternative methods. Our methods include statistical analyses of the following: applications for apprenticeship, referrals of qualified apprentices, actual employment of apprentices, employment on the METRO subway project, membership in local unions, and man-hours performed on federal construction sites, all by craft and by race. We believe that an increase in demand for minority craftsmen in the covered trades should be reflected in the racial makeup of apprentice programs, the largest construction project in the Washington area (METRO), federal construction sites, and in the referral unions themselves. By studying these indicators, we have made an effort to determine if the Washington Plan has had a substantial effect on the utilization of minorities in the construction industry. Although we cannot isolate the effects of other significant factors such as the Civil Rights Act and other laws, we can note changes in employment trends since the imposition of the Plan.

In order to supplement quantitative data, we have conducted an extensive survey of all parties interested in the Washington Plan issue: contractors, unions, the community, and the government. The bulk of Chapter VI will be devoted to the results of this survey. We have found that a qualitative search is a necessary part of any effort to evaluate an imposed plan since quantitative data alone do not tell the whole story. For example, changing attitudes are often equally as valuable by-products of an affirmative action program as the immediately realized changes in the number of minorities employed. Thus, it is hoped that the fruits of several months of field interviewing will provide an appropriate balance to the quantitative analysis presented below.

Apprenticeships

If the scarcity of skilled minorities is as serious as many contractors and union officials claim, it would be expected that a large percentage of those minorities hired for compliance purposes would be in the apprentice category. Organized labor has been emphatically stressing the importance of apprenticeship for entering minorities. In order to examine the effects of the Washington Plan on apprenticeship, information from the District of Columbia Manpower Administration, which maintains reliable data on applications, qualifications, referrals, and registrations in apprenticeship programs, was utilized. The specific agencies contacted were the D.C. Employment Services, Apprenticeship Information Center, and the D.C. Apprenticeship Council.

Table 7 outlines the overall activity of most construction apprenticeship programs registered with the D.C. Apprenticeship Council. The trades listed include not only the Washington Plan crafts, but others as well. The data presented are the absolute number of applicants for apprenticeship who were qualified, those who were referred to apprenticeship programs, and those who were ultimately accepted into a registered program. Because employers on occasion enter a youth into a probationary form of apprenticeship, the data probably understate the number of actual entries. Furthermore, the absolute figures must be viewed cautiously, since the attrition of new apprentices is often as high as 50 percent. Carpenters' union officials admit that over half of their apprentice classes will drop out before completing the program.

It is clear from Table 7 that during the period from January 1968 to May 1971, a period of over 40 months, there was no great influx of minorities into construction apprenticeship. The overall proportion of apprentices who were members of a minority group was much lower than the 26 percent proportion of minorities in the Washington SMSA. Although some trades do not register all of their apprentices with the D.C. Apprenticeship Council, the overall proportion of minority acceptances, 20.4 percent, is higher than that of the Washington Plan trades.

TABLE 7. *Washington Plan*
Washington, D.C. Apprenticeship Referrals and Acceptances
by Craft and Race
January 1968-May 1971 [a]

	Referrals			Acceptances		
	Total	Minority	Percent Minority	Total	Minority	Percent Minority
Electricians	721	150	20.8	242	29	12.0
Carpenters	702	218	31.1	509	125	24.6
Lathers	37	9	24.3	41	2	4.9
Operating Engineers	282	93	33.0	85	20	23.5
Sheet Metal Workers	340	105	30.9	128	21	16.4
Plumbers	252	82	32.5	114	27	23.7
Painters	79	42	53.2	27	6	22.2
Cement Finishers	55	43	78.2	18	15	83.3
Pipefitters	243	47	19.3	95	20	21.1
Steamfitters	26	3	11.5	103	11	10.7
Glaziers	3	1	33.3	3	0	—
Asbestos Workers	33	19	57.6	12	9	75.0
Ironworkers	48	29	60.4	11	0	—
Rodmen	1	0	—	9	0	—
Totals	2,822	841	29.8	1,397	285	20.4

Source: D.C. Employment Services form ES-239.

[a] Data for May 1969 and August 1969 were not available.

This is attributable in part to the inflationary effects of the cement finishers, operating engineers, and carpenters, all non-Washington Plan trades. Most trades, however, show a drop in the percentage of minorities from the referral stage to acceptance. This may reflect the results of the interview stage of hiring, since those referred should already meet the standard qualifications.

Tables 8 and 9 are more useful to our study. Table 8 presents referral and acceptance data for a one-year period prior to June 1970 when the Washington Plan was imposed and Table 9 outlines apprenticeship data for the year following that date. It is readily apparent that more apprenticeship registration activity occurred during the second half of this two-year period as total apprentice acceptances increased by 139.4 percent and minority apprentice acceptance increased by 246.3 percent during the first year of the Plan's imposition. The proportion of minorities in those trades listed increased overall from 14.8 percent to 21.4 percent.

The performance of each Washington Plan trade is another matter. The lathers, sheet metal workers, plumbers, pipefitters, steamfitters, and asbestos workers showed an increase in minority employment, but the electricians, painters, glaziers, and ironworkers demonstrated little or no progress.

The absolute number of minorities registered in apprenticeship programs exceeds the previous yearly total by over 200 percent, but the numbers are not large. In the craft categories covered by the Plan only sixty-three minorities were new entries into apprenticeship during the year following the beginning of the Washington Plan.

The data in tables 8 and 9 lend credence to the contention of some trades that lack of employment growth in their crafts will

TABLE 8. *Washington Plan*
Washington, D.C. Apprenticeship Referrals and Acceptances
by Craft and Race
June 1969-May 1970 [a]

	Referrals			Acceptances		
	Total	Minority	Percent Minority	Total	Minority	Percent Minority
Electricians	195	33	16.9	59	8	13.6
Carpenters	196	69	35.2	65	14	21.5
Lathers	2	2	100.0	1	0	—
Operating Engineers	74	29	39.2	21	0	—
Sheet Metal Workers	51	8	15.7	49	6	12.2
Plumbers	47	12	25.5	20	4	20.0
Painters	27	11	40.7	17	6	35.3
Cement Finishers	14	7	50.0	2	1	50.0
Pipefitters	52	5	9.6	26	2	7.7
Steamfitters	0	0	—	8	0	—
Glaziers	1	0	—	1	0	—
Asbestos Workers	2	0	—	0	0	—
Ironworkers	31	14	45.2	8	0	—
Rodmen	1	0	—	0	0	—
Totals	693	190	27.4	277	41	14.8

Source: D.C. Employment Services form ES-239.

[a] Data for August 1969 were not available.

TABLE 9. *Washington Plan*
Washington, D.C. Apprenticeship Referrals and Acceptances
by Craft and Race
June 1970-May 1971

	Referrals			Acceptances		
	Total	Minority	Percent Minority	Total	Minority	Percent Minority
Electricians	382	55	14.4	127	12	9.4
Carpenters	250	74	29.6	320	56	17.5
Lathers	3	3	100.0	1	1	100.0
Operating Engineers	124	43	34.7	31	10	32.3
Sheet Metal Workers	125	55	44.0	22	7	31.8
Plumbers	126	43	34.1	49	12	24.5
Painters	38	27	71.1	0	0	—
Cement Finishers	28	26	92.9	13	13	100.0
Pipefitters	93	22	23.7	58	17	29.3
Steamfitters	4	0	—	27	5	18.5
Glaziers	1	1	100.0	0	0	—
Asbestos Workers	27	19	70.4	12	9	75.0
Ironworkers	17	15	88.2	3	0	—
Rodmen	0	0	—	0	0	—
Totals	1,218	383	31.4	663	142	21.4

Source: D.C. Employment Services form ES-239.

severely hamper their efforts to change the color of their local unions. The lathers registered only two new apprentices of any race during the period June 1969 to June 1971. Similarly, the asbestos workers registered twelve, and the glaziers only one.

Some large trades have had surprisingly little apprenticeship activity. During the year following the imposition of the Plan, the painters registered no apprentices, the ironworkers only three, and the rodmen none. The latter, however, have had considerable success in upgrading laborers and thus may not rely on apprenticeship as a source of potential journeymen, as the skill level of rodmen is not high.

In sum, if apprenticeship registration is used as a measure of the response of the construction industry to the Washington Plan, it could be concluded that, despite variances from trade to trade, there has been an increase in the registration of minorities into apprenticeship since the Plan began. As shown in Tables 8 and 9, it is clear that the percentage of minorities entering apprenticeship in the listed covered trades (electricians, lathers, sheet metal workers, plumbers, painters, pipefitters, steamfitters, glaziers, asbestos workers, and ironworkers) increased from 13.7 percent during the year prior to the Plan to 21.1 percent in the year following its imposition. However, the actual number of minorities entering apprenticeship increased by only thirty-seven, to a total of sixty-three.

Tables 10 through 14 also indicate that blacks have been getting a growing share of the new apprenticeship openings in the construction industry. Undoubtedly, the Washington Plan must be credited with much of this improvement.

Table 10 indicates how applicants for apprenticeship fared during the entry process. In addition to the basic age, education, and physical requirements for entrance into a program, applicants are required to take the General Aptitude Test Battery (GATB) administered by the Apprenticeship Information Center. Throughout the period January 1968 through May 1971, over one-half of the applicants tested were minorities. Almost

TABLE 10. *Washington Plan*
Washington, D.C. Apprenticeships:
From Testing to Employment Sponsor, by Race
January 1968-May 1971

	Total	Black	Percent Black
Applicants Tested	6,265	3,221	51.4
Applicants Below the Norm for ATB	980	714	72.9
Applicants Qualified for Apprenticeship	5,372	2,766	51.5
Applicants Failing to Qualify a	851	620	72.9
Referrals to Apprenticeship Sponsors b	2,825	844	29.9
Applicants Acceptd for Employment by Sponsors b	1,397	285	20.4

Source: D.C. Employment Services form ES-239.

a Not included in those below norm.

b Applicants in these categories include some from previous periods.

three-quarters of the failures, however, were nonwhites. By the end of the application process, only 29.9 percent of those referred to apprenticeship programs were minorities. Finally, minorities comprised only 20.4 percent of the applicants accepted by the sponsors of the apprenticeship programs (union and/or employer). Thus, the attrition of minorities from application to acceptance is much higher than that of whites.

By examining the trend over time, however, one can see that the situation is changing in favor of increased minority entry. During the period June 1968 through May 1969, as the data in Table 11 demonstrate, only 15.6 percent of the applicants for construction apprenticeship actually accepted by program sponsors were minorities, although minorities constituted 27.4 percent of those qualified and referred to these programs. During the following twelve months, the situation remained the same, with a high percentage of minorities failing to qualify and those qualifying ultimately failing to be accepted (Table 12).

TABLE 11. *Washington Plan*
Washington, D.C. Apprenticeships:
From Testing to Employment Sponsor, by Race
June 1968-May 1969 [a]

	Total	Black	Percent Black
Applicants Tested	1,225	572	46.7
Applicants Below the Norm for ATB	334	237	71.0
Applicants Qualified for Apprenticeship	942	380	40.3
Applicants Failing to Qualify [b]	205	156	76.1
Referrals to Apprenticeship Sponsors [c]	532	156	27.4
Applicants Accepted for Employment by Sponsors [c]	417	65	15.6

Source: D.C. Employment Services form ES-239.

[a] Includes 11 months only; data for May 1969 were not available.

[b] Not included in those below norm.

[c] Applicants in these categories include some from previous periods.

TABLE 12. *Washington Plan*
Washington, D.C. Apprenticeships:
From Testing to Employment Sponsor, by Race
June 1969-May 1970 [a]

	Total	Black	Percent Black
Applicants Tested	1,117	506	45.3
Applicants Below the Norm for ATB	213	155	72.8
Applicants Qualified for Apprenticeship	819	327	39.9
Applicants Failing to Qualify [b]	188	147	78.2
Referrals to Apprenticeship Sponsors [c]	693	190	27.4
Applicants Accepted for Employment by Sponsors [c]	277	41	14.8

Source: D.C. Employment Services form ES-239.

[a] Includes 11 months only; data for August 1969 were not available.

[b] Not included in those below norm.

[c] Applicants in these categories include some from previous periods.

During the year following the imposition of the Plan, the situation apparently changed. In this year the numbers of minorities applying for apprenticeship jumped drastically; the absolute number of minorities increased fourfold (Table 13). Although the upsurge in applications reflected an improvement of economic conditions in the industry, the proportion of the applicants who were nonwhite had grown to 63.0 percent. There was a significant drop in the test failure rate for blacks; for the first time more whites failed the GATB than blacks. This may have resulted from improved test-taking preparation of minority applicants and a reevaluation of testing standards by unions and contractors. There may also have been some revisions of the tests, which have been frequently attacked as being biased against blacks.

TABLE 13. *Washington Plan*
Washington, D.C. Apprenticeships:
From Testing to Employment Sponsor, by Race
June 1970-May 1971

	Total	Black	Percent Black
Applicants Tested	3,248	2,047	63.0
Applicants Below the Norm for ATB	298	134	45.0
Applicant Qualified for Apprenticeship	2,912	1,735	59.6
Applicants Failing to Qualify [a]	289	183	63.3
Referrals to Apprenticeship Sponsors [b]	1,218	383	31.4
Applicants Accepted for Employment by Sponsors [b]	663	142	21.4

Source: D.C. Employment Services form ES-239.

[a] Not included in those below norm.

[b] Applicants in these categories include some from previous periods.

The proportion of those referred to apprenticeship sponsors also shows some improvement over the twelve months following the Plan. Between June 1970 and May 1971, over 30 percent of those qualified and referred were black. In addition, the gap between referral and acceptance appears to be closing, since 21.4 percent of those accepted in this period were black, in itself an improvement over the 14.8 percent of the previous year.

It appears that black apprentice candidates are becoming more acceptable to unions. Table 14, which contains data for the period from October 1970 through May 1971, shows that 32.9 percent of the applicants referred to apprenticeship programs were black. In regard to actual acceptance, the percentage for blacks was 30.2 percent. This indicates the smallest variation from referral to acceptance since at least January 1968, and most likely ever. Thus, we must conclude that contractors and union apprenticeship officials are becoming more willing to accept a minority applicant who meets apprenticeship qualifications.

Although other forces are undoubtedly still at work, the Washington Plan must have played a substantial part in bringing about this trend. Our analysis reveals that minorities are winning a larger share of apprenticeship openings. There has been progress in the trades registered with the D.C. Apprenticeship Council, but data comprising Tables 10 through 14 include

TABLE 14. *Washington Plan*
Washington, D.C. Apprenticeships:
From Testing to Employment Sponsor, by Race
October 1970-May 1971

	Total	Black	Percent Black
Applicants Tested	2,426	1,608	66.3
Applicants Below the Norm for ATB	235	95	40.4
Applicants Qualified for Apprenticeship	2,217	1,273	57.4
Applicants Failing to Qualify [a]	211	144	68.2
Referrals to Apprenticeship Sponsors [b]	838	276	32.9
Applicants Accepted for Employment by Sponsors [b]	371	112	30.2

Source: D.C. Employment Services form ES-239.

[a] Not included in those below norm.

[b] Applicants in these categories include some from previous periods.

some trades which have always had a high proportion of blacks, so that the performance of the covered trades may be somewhat weaker than that suggested by the overall figures presented. Data are also missing concerning the minority apprentice dropout rate, which is alleged to be quite high. Despite these caveats, however, the figures do indicate progress under the Plan.

A significant proportion of the minorities hired for the purpose of compliance with the Washington Plan are neither apprentices nor union journeymen. Minority travelers, permit holders, trainees, and those hired just to be present are being used to provide the minority man-hours necessary to avoid debarment. Travelers are union members from out of town who are hired for a short duration; permit holders are craftsmen who are not granted member status in the union but are allowed to work as long as the union renews their permits; trainees include preapprentices, who also lack job security; and the others are the occasional minorities who are placed on the payroll despite lack of experience.

METRO Employment

To indicate whether or not the minorities being brought on the job because of the Washington Plan are being given long range opportunity in the industry, the METRO subway system, the largest single construction project in the city, was examined. It must first be recognized that not all of the covered trades are yet employed on METRO projects. Throughout the first year of the Washington Plan, the primary trades employed on METRO projects were the laborers, carpenters, operating engineers, tunnelers, and teamsters, all trades excluded from the Plan.

Tables 15, 16, and 17 show the average monthly employment on METRO by race and trade for quarters ending April 1971, July 1971, and October 1971, respectively. During those quarters, the OFCC issued man-hour data for each of the covered trades on all federal sites in the form of a report to the Washington Plan Review Committee. These data and the controversy surrounding the reports will be presented below and later in this chapter.

TABLE 15. *Washington Plan*
Average Monthly Employment on METRO Construction
by Craft and Race
for Quarter Ending April 1971

Craft	Average Total	Average Minority	Percent Minority
Asbestos Workers	NA	NA	—
Boilermakers	NA	NA	—
Electricians	11.3	1.7	15.0
Elevator Constructors	NA	NA	—
Glaziers	5.3	0	0.0
Ironworkers	0	0	—
Painters	0	0	—
Plumbers	10.3	3	29.1
Pipefitters	5.3	5	94.3
Sheet Metal Workers	0	0	—
Steamfitters	NA	NA	—
Welder-Burners	10	3.3	33.3
Tile-Setters	NA	NA	—
Operating Engineers	136.3	23.7	17.4
Carpenters [a]	43.3	14.3	33.0

Source: METRO Monthly Utilization Reports.

[a] Does not include pilebutts although the carpenters organize this craft.

TABLE 16. *Washington Plan*
Average Monthly Employment on METRO Construction
by Craft and Race
for Quarter Ending July 1971

Craft	Average Total	Average Minority	Percent Minority
Asbestos Workers	NA	NA	—
Boilermakers	NA	NA	—
Electricians	10.3	2	19.4
Elevator Constructors	NA	NA	—
Glaziers	0	0	—
Ironworkers	1.7	.7	41.2
Painters	.7	.7	100.0
Plumbers	8.7	2.7	31.0
Pipefitters	6.7	6.3	94.0
Sheet Metal Workers	2	.3	15.0
Steamfitters	NA	NA	—
Welder-Burners	5	1	20.0
Tile-Setters	NA	NA	—
Operating Engineers	174.7	35.7	20.4
Carpenters [a]	64.3	14	21.8

Source: METRO Monthly Utilization Reports.

[a] Does not include pilebutts although the carpenters organize this craft.

TABLE 17. *Washington Plan*
Average Monthly Employment on METRO Construction
by Craft and Race
for Quarter Ending October 1971

Craft	Average Total	Average Minority	Percent Minority
Asbestos Workers	NA	NA	—
Boilermakers	NA	NA	—
Electricians	32.7	8.3	25.4
Elevator Constructors	NA	NA	—
Glaziers	0	0	—
Ironworkers	9	3.3	36.7
Painters	0	0	—
Plumbers	1	.7	70.0
Pipefitters	6.3	4	63.5
Sheet Metal Workers	1	.7	70.0
Steamfitters	NA	NA	—
Welder-Burners	18.7	5.3	28.3
Tile-Setters	0	0	—
Operating Engineers	73.0	13.7	18.8
Carpenters [a]	285.3	49.3	17.3

Source: METRO Monthly Utilization Reports.

[a] Does not include pilebutts although the carpenters organize this craft.

The electricians, ironworkers, plumbers, pipefitters, and welders (steamfitters) are the only covered trades significantly employed on METRO sites. It is obvious, however, that most of the skilled minorities have been employed in the carpenter and operating engineer categories. The electricians and the plumber/pipefitters appear to be increasing their preference for minorities. The ironworkers have been employing a high proportion of minorities, but the average employment on METRO in this trade has been low.

The two large trades specifically excluded from the Plan are the operating engineers and the carpenters. Approximately 19 percent of the employed operating engineers are minorities, but the carpenters, on the other hand, have allowed the proportion of minorities employed to slip while more and more carpenters are brought onto METRO sites. The average monthly employment of carpenters during the quarter ending April 1971 was 43.3; 33.0 percent of those were minorities. By the quarter ending October 1971, the average monthly employment had risen to 285.3. Contractors were apparently unable to fill many of the new openings with minorities, since the proportion of minorities had fallen to 17.3 percent.

In order to examine the performance of each Washington Plan craft over time as the goals escalate, a time series regression was employed on selected trades employed on METRO and corresponding apprenticeship entries. If new minorities are entering the trades through the apprenticeship route, as many of the unions seemed to demand, then there should be some similarity between the employment trends on METRO and the appropriate apprenticeship program. It should be recalled that, according to the racial makeup of those referred and accepted into apprenticeship, there has been an improvement in favor of increased minority entry.

Although it is understood that fluctuations in employment on METRO are primarily the result of changing construction needs, we have found high positive correlations with time in the employment of minorities by plumbing and electrical subcontractors, in the total employment of carpenters, and in both the total and minority utilization of operating engineers (see Table 18). The data analyzed cover a period of fourteen months.

There is almost negligible correlation with time in apprenticeship entries over the thirty-nine months examined. The need for apprentices fluctuates widely and the time of acceptance is

TABLE 18. *Washington Plan*
Comparison of Correlation Coefficients of Regression Analysis
between METRO Employment
and Apprenticeship Referrals and Acceptances
for Selected Trades [a]

| | METRO EMPLOYMENT | | | | APPRENTICESHIP [b] | | | |
| | Prime Contractor | | Subcontractor | | Referrals | | Acceptances | |
	Total	Minority	Total	Minority	Total	Minority	Total	Minority
Plumbers	.4472	.4472	.7911	.6671	.3064	.3311	.0031	.0045
Electricians	.3922	c	.7759	.8348	.4028	.1751	.1192	d
Carpenters	.8193	.2697	.6645	.4017	.1282	.0755	.2636	.3945
Operating Engineers	.9682	.9724	.1123	.1502	.2499	.2628	.0196	.0686

Source: D.C. Employment Services form ES-239 and METRO Monthly Utilization Reports.

[a] Each classification was run as a time series. Data spans are: METRO n=14 months; Apprentice n=39 months.

[b] Regressions for the last year produce correlations which are poor.

[c] Data points are all zero.

[d] Not run but the correlation would be very poor.

Note: Measures exist to determine whether the correlation coefficients shown in this table are significantly different than zero. These measures have not been calculated because the data did not permit strong conclusions. The table is presented here, as noted in the text, as a method of evaluation which will prove more useful as METRO construction progresses.

often restricted to certain months, depending on the trade. What is important, however, is that although minority employment in the two METRO crafts is rising steadily with time, apprenticeship entry for minorities is not. It may be that those minorities gaining METRO employment are in classifications other than apprentice or journeyman, the two union-member categories.

We hesitate to draw any strong conclusions from our analysis of METRO data. There is no question that the METRO system employs many minorities but most are concentrated in the lower skilled categories. Unfortunately, too few crafts are as yet employed to permit an evaluation of METRO's final impact. When the stations begin to go up and the tunnels are finished, the METRO system should become a better indicator of the industry's response to the Washington Plan. At that time, the methodology set forth here should lend significant results in determining whether METRO employment under the Washington Plan aegis is having a significant long-term effect.

Minority Man-hours on Federal Sites

The most frequently used measure of the performance of Washington Plan trades is the minority utilization data on federal construction sites. As required by the Plan, OFCC reports the progress of the Plan to the Washington Plan Review Committee, a group made up of representatives of the industry, organized labor, community, and government.

Quarterly reports are developed from the minority utilization reports prepared monthly by Washington Plan contractors, sent to contracting agencies, and forwarded to OFCC. The data presented in the quarterly reports include total and minority man-hours by trade and agency plus overall percentage performance by each trade. These reports do not contain minority utilization on private sites, although the Plan requires company-wide compliance.[74]

Because of statistical errors, confusing format, and incomplete data, these reports are somewhat less than a true measure of the Plan's performance. It is fair to say, however, that since a complete accounting of all those hired because of the Plan does not exist, these reports are a better measure of progress than apprentice registrations or employment on METRO, and therefore the best available.

Tables 19 through 21 are based on quarterly reports presented to the Washington Plan Review Committee. The total and minority man-hours performed in each covered trade as employed by both union and nonunion contractors are compiled and the overall percentages given. Although compliance is judged on a contractor basis, overall percentages have been compared with the goals established for the appropriate year. Table 22 makes such a comparison for two quarters. From this comparison one could conclude that many of the trades are meeting their goals. According to the report covering the period August through September 1971, the asbestos workers, elevator constructors, glaziers, lathers, painters, and sheet metal workers were below

---

[74] A more detailed evaluation of these reports is presented later in this chapter.

TABLE 19. *Washington Plan*
Minority Manpower Utilization on Federal Construction Projects
Reported by All Contracting Agencies to OFCC
Quarter Ending April 1791

Trade	Total Man-hours	Minority Man-hours	Percent Minority
Asbestos Workers	8,959	2,280	25.4
Boilermakers	0	0	—
Electricians	59,806	10,920	18.3
Elevator Constructors	254	0	—
Glaziers	1,859	0	—
Ironworkers	54,736	11,015	20.1
Lathers	24	2	8.3
Painters	5,222	915	17.5
Plumbers and Pipefitters	26,505	1,535	5.8 [a]
Sheet Metal Workers	24,831	2,482	10.0
Steamfitters	20,859	2,900	13.9
Tile & Terrazzo Workers	257	0	—

Source: "Status Report on Washington Plan," OFCC, June 7, 1971 and
Department of Labor, News Release, USDL—71-319, June 10, 1971.
[a] The memorandum and news release incorrectly reported this figure as 11.58 percent.

TABLE 20. *Washington Plan*
Minority Manpower Utilization on Federal Construction Projects
Reported by All Contracting Agencies to OFCC
Quarter Ending July 1971

Trade	Total Man-hours	Minority Man-hours	Percent Minority
Asbestos Workers	42,323	5,169	12.2
Boilermakers	0	0	—
Electricians	118,166	21,384	18.1
Elevator Constructors	3,331	680	20.4
Glaziers	1,027	73	7.1
Ironworkers	27,789	4,932	17.7
Lathers	0	0	—
Painters	1,621	532	32.8
Plumbers and Pipefitters	134,593	25,446	18.9
Sheet Metal Workers	54,695	4,689	8.6
Steamfitters	53,122	7,372	13.9
Tile & Terrazzo Workers	1,210	828	68.4 [a]

Source: "Status Report on Washington Plan," OFCC, September 23, 1971.
[a] The memorandum incorrectly reported this figure as 0 percent.

TABLE 21. *Washington Plan*
Minority Manpower Utilization on Federal Construction Projects
Reported by All Contracting Agencies to OFCC
Quarter Ending October 1971

Trade	Total Man-hours	Minority Man-hours	Percent Minority
Asbestos Workers	45,726	4,766	10.4
Boilermakers	0	0	—
Electricians	180,097	43,625	24.2
Elevator Constructors	7,202	1,402	19.5
Glaziers	2,717	230	8.5
Ironworkers	34,839	9,779	28.1
Lathers	4,977	648	13.0
Painters	41,491	8,477	20.4
Plumbers and Pipefitters	211,861	45,060	21.3
Sheet Metal Workers	93,139	9,284	10.0
Steamfitters	37,117	6,184	16.7
Tile & Terrazzo Workers	3,821	1,176	30.8

Source: "Status Report on Washington Plan," OFCC, December 14, 1971.

the goals set for May 1972, yet had time to reach compliance.[75] By the first deadline of May 1971, however, only two trades were below the minimum goals.

Examination of Tables 19 through 22 reveals great fluctuations in the employment of each trade from quarter to quarter. The trades with the lowest levels of employment show the most dramatic changes. The tile and terrazzo workers went from 0 percent to 68.4 percent to 30.8 percent over the three quarters.

These reports are most useful in assessing how the proportion of minorities employed varies with the changes in overall employment. It is obvious that when the total employed is relatively low, the crafts have been better able to meet the Washington Plan goals. An increase of one black worker to a declining or low total employment figure increases minority man-hours to a greater degree than the addition of one black worker to an increasing or high total employment figure. This fact is con-

---

[75] The actual period covered by this particular report is uncertain. The report itself cites August-September as the period covered, yet all others have covered a full quarter.

TABLE 22. *Washington Plan*
Overall Progress of the Washington Plan as Reported to
the Washington Plan Review Committee by OFCC

	First Year		Second Year		
	Percent Minority Utilization Through April 1971	Required Percentage Goal Range through May 1971	Percent Minority Utilization May-June 1971	Percent Minority Utilization August-September 1971	Required Percentage Goal Range through May 1971
Asbestos Workers	25.4	8-14	12.2	10.4'	14-20
Boilermakers	a	6-12	—	—	12-18
Electrical Workers	18.3	10-16	18.1	24.2	16-22
Elevator Constructors	0	16-22	20.4	19.5	22-28
Glaziers	0	10-16	7.1	8.5	16-22
Iron Workers	20.1	11-19	17.7	28.1	19-27
Lathers	8.3	16-22	—	13.0	22-28
Painters	17.5	14-21	32.8	20.4	21-28
Plumbers and Pipefitters	5.8	10-15	18.9	21.3	15-20
Sheet Metal Workers	10.0	7-13	8.6	10.0	13-19
Steamfitters	13.9	10-15	13.9	16.7	15-20
Tile and Terrazzo Workers	0	10-16	68.4	30.8	16-22

Source: Tables 19, 20, 21 and the Washington Plan.
a 0 man hours in covered time period.

firmed below by our finding that minorities are not being left on the bench when contractors need them for compliance purposes.

The asbestos workers show continued difficulty in meeting their goals; in fact, the proportion of minorities employed decreased at a time when overall employment in this trade doubled on federal sites.

The boilermakers are totally unaffected by the Plan since they are not employed on any covered contracts. The electricians, however, are showing much progress. The overall utilization of minorities has increased during a rapid increase of overall employment in this trade.

Although the elevator constructors have actually employed few minorities, they appear to be making a concerted effort to increase their minority man-hours on federal projects. Similarly, the glaziers show some progress but the actual employment of minorities is quite small.

The demand for ironworkers fluctuates considerably, but if one uses minority man-hours as a measure of success, the overall goals have been met. The lathers have had compliance difficulties despite an extremely low level of overall employment.

The painters provide a good example of how the minority percentage depends on overall employment. When total man-hours dropped from 5,222 to 1,621, minority utilization rose from 17.5 percent to 32.8 percent (Tables 19 and 20). The increase may have been due to reluctance on the part of contractors to take minorities off the more visible federal sites.

The plumbers and pipefitters, who comprise one reporting category, have been able to meet the Plan's goals overall. It is apparent from apprenticeship information presented earlier in this chapter that the majority of the minority entries are from the pipefitter category. The increase in employment of these pipetradesmen in the summer of 1971 did not diminish the minority utilization rate on federal projects.

The sheet metal workers have maintained a steady, but low proportion of minority employees. As the goals escalate they should have greater difficulty in meeting the Plan's requirements.

The steamfitters have also remained somewhat constant, with the greatest increase in the minority proportion coming when overall employment of this trade declined. Finally, the tile and terrazzo workers have demonstrated the ability to comply with the goals overall since the actual total of man-hours performed is quite low.

These reports make it clear that minorities are being hired as a result of the compliance pressure of the Washington Plan. Unfortunately, the percentages set forth in the compliance reports do not tell us the nature of the employment of those minorities allegedly hired because of the Washington Plan. The construction industry is characterized by casual employment with employers constantly adjusting the size of their work force, often on a weekly basis. The quarterly man-hour reports which are used as an informal measure of evaluation by OFCC do not measure how much the Plan has done to achieve long-range opportunity for minorities in construction. To answer in part the question of whether or not minorities are achieving permanent attachment to the work force, it is necessary to examine union membership information.

Union Membership

Table 23 is the product of our survey of the union locals representing the trades covered by the Washington Plan. It is based on interviews with each local. This table may overstate the percentages of minorities who are actually full members because trainees, helpers, and permit holders may have been included by business agents in their figures.

A comparison of Tables 23 and 24 shows how great the discrepancy is between the man-hour percentages and the actual participation of minorities in organized labor. In every case, the proportion of minorities who are union members is far below that presented in the Washington Plan Review Committee reports. In fact, only one union of all covered trades has a minority membership in excess of 10 percent. This is the key argument of community leaders: How can there really be compliance with the Washington Plan when none of the unions have a membership which equals the proportion of minorities in the whole country, much less in a city that is over 71 percent black?

We can only conclude that compliance has been achieved in many cases through the use of travelers, permit holders, trainees, and others who may gain some beneficial on-the-job experience. Whether they will eventually gain the benefits of union membership as a result of the Washington Plan remains to be demonstrated.

TABLE 23. *Washington Plan*
Union Membership by Race, 1971

	Membership			Journeymen			Apprentices		
	Total	Minority	Percent Minority	Total	Minority	Percent Minority	Total	Minority	Percent Minority
Asbestos Workers, Local 224	329	11	3.3	263	2	0.8	66	9	13.6
Boilermakers, Local 193	291	1	0.3	250	0	0.0	41	1	2.4
IBEW, Local 26	1,500 a	96	6.4	NA	70	—	NA	26	—
Elevator Constructors, Local 10	640 b	18 b	2.8	540	4 c	0.7	100 d	14 e	14.0
Glaziers, Local 963	226	11	4.9	206	6	2.9	20	5	25.0
Ironworkers, Local 5	628 f	45	7.2	550	35 g	6.4	78	10	12.8
Lathers, Local 9	125	11	8.8	120	6	5.0	5	5	100.0
Painters, District Council	1,129	121	10.7	1,108	113	10.2	21	8	38.1
Plumbers, Local 5	910	65	7.1	785	25	3.2	125	40	32.0
Sheet Metal Workers, Local 102	875	28	3.2	725	5	0.7	150	23	15.3
Steamfitters, Local 502	989	97	9.8	766	54	7.0	223	43	19.3
Tile and Terrazzo Workers, Local 3	122	9	7.4	122	9 h	7.4	0	0	—

Source: Field survey 1971.

a Included are 56 black trainees. A further breakdown was not available.

b Mechanics, helpers, and permit holders.

c Mechanics and helpers.

d Permit holders.

e Permit holders working as helpers.

f Not included are 14 black advanced trainees.

g Includes 30 S.S.A. and American Indians.

h Includes one Cuban.

TABLE 24. *Washington Plan*

A Comparison Between Minority Representation in Washington, D.C. Construction Locals and Minority Utilization on Federal Projects in the Washington SMSA 1971-1972

| | Union Membership | | | | Total Membership | | | Washington Plan Man-Hours [a] | | |
| | Journeymen | | Apprentices | | | | | | | |
	Total	Minority	Total	Minority	Total	Minority	Percent Minority	Percent Minority May-July 1971	Percent Minority Aug.-Sept. 1971	Percent Required by May 31, 1972
Asbestos Workers	263	2	66	9	329	11	3.3	12.2	10.4	14-20
Boilermakers [b]	250	0	41	1	291	1	0.3	—	—	12-18
Electrical Workers [b]	1,500	70	NA	26	1,500	96	6.4	18.1	24.2	16-22
Elevator Constructor [c]	540	4	NA	NA	540	4	0.7	20.4	19.5	22-28
Glaziers	206	6	20	5	226	11	4.9	7.1	8.5	16-22
Iron Workers [d]	550	35	78	10	628	45	7.2	17.7	28.1	19-27
Lathers	120	6	5	5	125	11	8.8	—	13.0	22-28
Painters [e]	1,108	113	21	8	1,129	121	10.7	32.8	20.4	21-28
Plumbers & Pipefitters	785	25	125	40	910	65	7.1	18.9	21.3	15-20
Sheet Metal Workers [f]	725	5	150	23	875	28	3.2	8.6	10.0	13-19
Steamfitters	766	54	223	43	989	97	9.8	13.9	16.7	15-20
Tile & Terrazzo Workers [g]	122	9	0	0	122	9	7.4	68.4	30.8	16-22

Source: Tables 22 and 23.

[a] As per Washinton Plan; includes both union and nonunion work.
[b] Does not include 56 black trainees.
[c] Does not include 100 permit holders, 14 of which are black. Does include helpers.
[d] Does not include 14 black advanced trainees.
[e] Figures are same as those collected by the mayor's office, where we were referred for data.
[e] Figures are same as those collected by the Mayor's Office, where we were
[f] May include some permit holders.
[g] Does not include tile and terrazzo helpers' union.

Other measures of performance exist. OFCC could provide statistics on the number of contractors who have been found out of compliance, but since compliance has in all cases been achieved through good faith effort, definitive judgment cannot be made. Three of the four measures presented above, if taken together, can give a reasonably good picture of the performance of an imposed plan: apprentice registrations, man-hours on federal sites (and on private sites, hopefully), and union membership. Such an evaluation, however, cannot be readily routinized and even if accomplished will not tell the whole story.

In order to make the more difficult qualitative evaluation of the Washington Plan, extensive research and field interviews have been conducted. The results of this effort complete our assessment of the Washington Plan as it affects the industry, organized labor, community, and government.

CHAPTER VI

The Washington Plan in Practice: Problems and Progress

Since the Washington Plan places the burden of compliance on the contractor rather than on the union, our research began with a close look at contractors, their associations, and other elements of the industry. Although the nonunion contractor conducts an estimated 60 to 80 percent of all the construction activity in the Washington SMSA, our focus will remain on the union sector, which dominates the federally funded, heavy construction market.[76] The nonunion contractor is primarily involved with the building of schools, apartments, residences, and shopping centers, almost all uncovered by the Washington Plan's goals and timetables.

We have not omitted the nonunion sector from our analysis. Nevertheless, in the absence of any data which can place a percentage figure on the portion of federal construction held by union and nonunion firms, we estimate that as much as 90 percent of the Washington Plan contracts are awarded to union firms. With METRO subway costs ranging into billions of dollars and construction projects of the magnitude of the new FBI headquarters going to union firms, the Plan will have its greatest impact on the union sector.

Executive Order No. 11246, under which the Plan was developed, does not authorize direct regulation of the union hiring hall. The drafters of the Plan hope that by exerting pressure on union contractors, many of whom would go out of business without federal contracts, unions in turn would be compelled to open their doors to minorities. Furthermore, it was hoped that the escalating demands would create new opportunities for those already in training and that skilled minorities would be attracted from other professions. Our task has been to determine how contractors have responded to the goal pressures, whether the unions have in fact opened their doors wider, and if the escalating

---

[76] Based on estimates of contractor and association officials.

requirements for compliance have succeeded in providing greater opportunity for those in and outside of the construction industry.

Ironically, while the initial burden of compliance falls on the contractor, attention must be paid to the response of the countless subcontractors, for few prime contractors directly hire those crafts under regulation because of the Plan. Most of the prime contractors (general contractors) retain only laborers, carpenters, and some others as members of their permanent work force. Sheet metal workers, electricians, plumbers, tile workers, lathers, boilermakers, steamfitters, painters, asbestos workers, elevator constructors, iron workers, and glaziers are almost always provided by small subcontractors whose work forces may range from one to several hundred. The Washington Plan does not hold the general contractor accountable for subcontractor performance under its requirements as long as the general contractor has exerted a good faith effort to insure that his subcontractors alhere to the goals set for those trades.

The Compliance Process

In many cases, completing the Appendix A for each contract bid consists of agreeing to meet the minimum percentage goal of the ranges set for the crafts involved. Many general contractors write in these minimum goals and ask their subcontractors to meet the figures. Some contractors admit that it simply becomes a case of agreeing to the goals in order to get the contract and then later worrying about finding the needed minorities. If a contractor is later found to be not in compliance, he is asked to demonstrate to the contracting agency why he should not be debarred from further contracts. Such a summons is in the form of a "show cause" letter. OFCC enters if action is not taken by the agency. Since the beginning of the Washington Plan, dozens of firms have been issued show cause letters but most, apparently, have demonstrated sufficient good faith effort to avoid debarment. No contractor to date has been debarred in Washington. In fact, one contractor clearly admitted satisfying a show cause order for lack of compliance by shifting minority employees to the federal site in question.

Although the moving of blacks from site to site ahead of compliance officers is hardly a common practice, contractors and unions are quickly learning to manage their minority resources. Concentrated employment of minorities in one of the critical trades for only a short period of time may be sufficient to meet the goals of the Plan. In the union sector, minority workers can be rapidly referred to another contractor to repeat the experience. Our union survey confirms that, despite unemployemnt in some unions, minorities in the unions are rarely unemployed. Such favoritism may be seen as a positive sign that minorities are at last being insured skilled work, but we offer the possibility that relatively few minorities are being used to meet man-hour goals, and that permit holders—not new union members—are being used to meet the requirements of the Plan. This reduces the economic impact of the Plan on the black community and does not help to reduce the distrust many minorities feel for the building trades.

Either because of vigorous enforcement by the contracting agency or as a result of a show cause letter, several contractors have hired marginally qualified minorities merely to satisfy the man-hour requirements of an approaching deadline. In general, compliance officials do not investigate the basic qualifications of those brought in for compliance; they are certainly not required to do so. Last minute hiring to avoid debarment often proves to be a very short-range solution. This practice is in no way extensive but is another reaction by the industry to vigorous enforcement. The data presented in Chapter V confirm that last minute employment is merely a stop-gap measure. We found that no union in the Washington SMSA had a minority participation rate greater than 10 percent. The marginally employed minority is not a union member and, therefore, has no claim on future work.

There are signs that the Washington Plan has reduced the number of bids for subcontracting work. Small subcontractors, who are unwilling to make drastic changes in their work force, will not bid on short duration work. In order to comply with the Plan, some small subcontractors would only have to employ one or two minorities for a matter of days. Unless these blacks are members of a union, the wisdom of such action is highly questionable. Who would apply for work under such an arrangement? Most often the subcontractor cannot do otherwise, for once the short subcontract is completed, there may be little work for the newly employed. As the goals escalate over time, however, small contractors will be less able to be so selective in bidding. More and more of them will find present work force makeups inadequate to meet the required goals. Evidence of this potential squeeze is seen in the increasing incidence of prime contractors passing over low subcontractor bids in order to get complying subcontractors.

Construction costs and minority employment could both increase over time.

Finally, the lack of communication with the government over compliance problems has become a sore spot with Washington contractors. Many of those interviewed felt that the percentage ranges should be reviewed (as provided in the Plan), yet were reluctant to challenge the existing goals without substantial statistical support. The Washington Plan Review Committee meetings, though continually attended by industry representatives, are not viewed as an effective means for working out valid problems. Throughout our survey, contractors were asked, "If you had a problem regarding the Plan, whom would you call?" Only a very few recognized that OFCC was directly involved in administering the Plan. Even fewer could name an individual to contact. The vast majority replied that they had no idea, other than the contracting agency involved. Almost all of those interviewed desired some central contact point for resolution of Washington Plan problems.

COMMUNITY

Exclusion from the lucrative skilled construction crafts has long been the focus of community anger in a city with a black majority. Federal dollars have been continually flowing to union contractors whose work forces reflect decades of exclusion from all but the lower paying trades. While other industries have been equally guilty of discrimination, construction has drawn attention because of its high pay, visibility, and long range opportunities for work near the communities where large numbers of Negroes dwell.

Washington Area Construction Industry Task Force

After the riots in the late 1960s, members of the community began discussing ways to enable blacks to take part in rebuilding their city. Leading community organizations attempted to coordinate the heretofore fragmented effort, with the Washington Urban League assuming leadership in forming a minority coalition to bring pressure more effectively to bear on the government, industry, and organized labor. Representatives from contractors groups, community organizations, unions, churches, schools, and other groups concerned with the problem met to form the Washington Area Construction Industry Task Force (WACITF). Throughout the first METRO controversy and the development of the Washington Plan, WACITF assumed the position of community representative. The Task Force successfully brought attention to the exclusion of minorities through its militancy and public exposure.

In retrospect, it appears that the development of a voluntary solution was impossible in Washington, given the brief time period available for negotiations. If OFCC had allowed more time for further efforts at the development of a hometown plan, however, a workable plan would have still been unlikely, given the individuals involved. A cooperative spirit between organized labor and contractors has existed, but an industry-wide plan would not have been possible without a deeply rooted representation of the community. Task Force representatives felt that any voluntary plan would result in only limited progress. A government imposed plan, in their eyes, could be no worse. Thus, they made demands that were unacceptable to industry.

The organization of the community is a primary ingredient for successful social action. In Washington, despite the formation of the Task Force, there were, and still are, few signs of broad-based community organization. One year after the imposition of the Plan most of the energy of the Task Force has been dissipated. Community leaders have moved on to other issues, thereby ending the concentration of minority voices which helped publicize the issue in 1970. There is controversy over whether WACITF leaders had the best interests of the community in mind when they presented the community position.

Many of the community spokesmen interviewed confirmed that a hometown solution would never be possible in Washington. First, there was no precedent for community-union or community-industry cooperation. There are minorities active in organized labor and in the construction industry, but a cooperative effort to end well-entrenched patterns of exclusion was not likely to develop. Second, the community itself was not sufficiently unified to provide unanimity or coordinated effort. Some of the WACITF spokesmen were recent arrivals in Washington who had achieved status in national politics. Third, there was no recognized community leader. Each organization had its own leaders, but few of those interviewed could agree on a strong spokesman capable of representing community interests in a coalition. Our experience suggests that only a strong community coalition would allow hometown negotiation of an affirmative action plan that would act in the community interest.

Other Community Agencies

Throughout our research, we found a multitude of black organizations striving to place more minorities in the construction industry. The Urban League, Opportunities Industrialization Center (OIC), and PRIDE, Inc. are but a few. Local community groups, business groups, and many offices of the District government are led by blacks who seek to train minority youths for careers in construction. Various forums, such as the biweekly meetings of the Mayor's Task Force on Construction Problems, bring community representatives together to address this continuing problem. The federal government spends large sums of money on many programs intended to train minorities in the construction crafts. What we found, in essence, was a massive, but totally fragmented, effort to place more minorities in a basically well-organized industry. Community groups, lacking the resources or a commitment by the industry to hire its referrals, sent minorities off to frequent rejection and greater frustration. We found that the only successful channels of minority placement are those that developed through years of dealing with the same individual or organization. Much of the limited success in placing minorities has come through this informal approach, as individuals in community organizations and the government have nourished contacts in the industry and with the unions to meet some of the community and industry manpower needs.

The Urban League

The Washington Urban League has long been involved in the construction issue. The Urban League maintains that there exists a large pool of qualified minorities who possess the skills and desire to be construction craftsmen. Only exclusion, it believes, prevents minorities from participating more fully in this industry. The Urban League hopes to develop a skills bank in which files on available minorities could be maintained. Since considerable emphasis has been placed on OJT as a means to employment for minorities who possess the necessary aptitude but are unable to enter through apprenticeship routes, the Urban League works with veterans and other unemployed minorities who may have the ability to become construction craftsmen. Urban League spokesmen indicate that they will strive to improve vocational school training and seek ways to win union or contractor hiring guarantees for graduates.

The Urban League is perhaps the foremost community organization involved in the Washington Plan issue. Its leaders represent community interests on the Washington Plan Review Committee. As noted above, however, efforts are not concentrated on this particular issue and other areas of discrimination certainly warrant their attention. In the absence of continued involvement by the Urban League, or other community groups, the government has assumed the role of community representative, with only limited success.

PRIDE and OIC

PRIDE, Inc., another community organization interested in the construction issue, has become less involved since the imposition of the Washington Plan. Recently, however, PRIDE's Director, elected to the District school board, has shown a strong interest in improving vocational education, a poorly utilized source of minority manpower.

OIC, on the other hand, has had more direct involvement with the Washington Plan. OIC has been contacted for minority apprentice applicants by contractors under pressure from the Plan. Recently, when an elevator firm requested apprentice candidates, OIC sent eight blacks to the elevator constructors' union for testing. Only one passed the test, and he was later disqualified for other reasons. Elevator contractors continue to work with OIC to find minorities acceptable to the union. The servicing of METRO escalators, for example, offers one area of opportunity.

Similarly, nonunion contractors with the Associated Builders and Contractors have found OIC a good source of minority applicants. Placements based on contractors' initiatives have not been impeded by union requirements.

The only previously exclusionary union which has shown an increased interest in cooperating with OIC has been IBEW, Local 26. In general, however, representatives of the OIC see the unions and discriminatory testing mechanisms as the primary bars to increased placement success.

Like Project BUILD, the OIC program provides testing, technical, and social training. OIC also maintains a followup service to keep in contact with their placements. OIC, however, does not seem to be greatly affected by the Washington Plan. Although interest in OIC's services has increased in a few areas because of the Plan, OIC placements have not dramatically increased. They suffer, as do other community organizations, from a high rejection rate of program graduates who are sent to unions or contractors for work. Although some discrimination exists, one reason for the high number of failures is the lack of understanding of union or contractor entry requirements. More community-industry communications would prevent the referral of obviously unqualified candidates. We do not deny that some entry requirements are often intentionally discriminatory, but not all candidates are rejected on strictly racial grounds. A wide gulf in understanding continues to exist.

The Demand for Labor-Community Response

One of the most important areas for our research was the response of the community to the demand for minorities created by the Washington Plan. Throughout the preimposition hearings, and in the text of the Washington Plan itself, there was much discussion of the alleged pool of minorities available to meet contractors' Plan requirements. Throughout our field work we searched for this pool. We asked community leaders, "If I were a contractor under the Washington Plan, where would I go to recruit minorities and fulfill my obligations?" Many pointed out that this was a contractor's, not the community's responsibility. The existence of a large supply of minority labor, however, was stated as a fact. Nonunion minority craftsmen, veterans, vocational school graduates, mechanics in related trades, and many others were cited as sources. As one community leader said in a television interview, "There are a number of blacks available. Our answer to the fact of finding black people, minority workers, to work in the construction industry is not a problem. . . . There are a number of black people working . . . within the Washington area that are working on jobs other than those in which they're qualified." [77] Exclusion was and still is given as the reason for this underutilization of minority skills.

Our finding is that such a pool probably does exist but will not provide an effective source of minority manpower for Washington Plan construction. The Plan has created the demand for minority craftsmen, but the existence of an affirmative action program alone is insufficient to change a well-entrenched opinion held by minorities that construction is exclusionary and offers no career for them.

We have found many cases of minority craftsmen who possess all the skills and intelligence necessary to meet union and con-

[77] "Community Tieline," WRC-TV, February 8, 1970.

tractors' requirements for entry. These craftsmen sense the increased demand for minorities in the construction trades, but because of the lack of demonstration that the Plan, the government, or changing attitudes will guarantee long-term opportunity in such a seasonal and cyclical industry, they will not leave their present jobs, no matter how low paying they may be. Few would risk quitting a government or even a supermarket job for the prospect of gaining only a permit to work, trainee status, or apprenticeship, all of which offer no guarantee against being unemployed weeks later. Even the high pay of the skilled trades is insufficient incentive, for security and freedom from discrimination are more important.

In addition, those minorities most able to have successful careers in construction are often dissuaded from seeking construction employment by members of their own race. Counselors, teachers, community leaders, and family all advise the promising young black to enter college, work for the government, or find white collar work. Construction is seen as laborer's work and white man's territory. There is evidence that blacks "are more apt to perceive barriers to entrance into apprenticeship" and that "principals and counselors [are] not giving as much information and encouragement concerning apprenticeship training to Negro students." [78]

In sum, the Washington Plan has indeed created demand for minorities, but those responding to job openings or those being referred by community groups and training programs are predominantly undereducated, undertrained, unemployed, and lack continued work experience. Without increased involvement of the total community and better visibility of the Washington Plan's successes, affirmative action efforts will continue to be frustrating for minorities and contractors alike. While the Plan may achieve the social goal of employing some unemployed, the target of the Plan, the skilled minority labor supply, remains essentially unmoved.

Our findings suggest that many aspects of a hometown plan are needed in Washington. Greater involvement of community leaders, more publicity, and continuous exchange of community and industry needs are missing elements in the administration of the Plan. The Washington Plan Review Committee could be the ve-

---

[78] Dr. Alfred S. Drew, *Educational and Training Adjustments in Selected Apprenticeable Trades* (Vol. II Appendices), Final Report Submitted to Manpower Administration, Office of Manpower Research, U.S. Department of Labor, November 1969, p. 5.

hicle for a new approach to the problem. A full discussion of this committee is presented below.

Demand vs. Supply: Continuing Problems

The construction industry will continue to have problems in recruiting skills blacks and other minorities. It shares part of the blame, as the image of the "hard hat" will be difficult to change. It appears that an extensive advertising campaign, similar to that found successful in attracting black police recruits, will be necessary. As one community leader described the situation: Something must be done to improve the public image of the construction industry; blacks have been kept out too long to just open the gates to employment now.

Many of the blacks interviewed indicate that they fear harassment in a previously all-white trade. The use of government power to force change by a union or contractor raises racial tensions. Thus many well-motivated blacks will take white collar jobs, for less than half the pay and none of the extra benefits, rather than do construction work which is either tension-filled or perceived as degrading.

Another barrier to the construction trades is the educational system, which places high value on college and little value on manual labor. Many blacks, as well as whites, see vocational training as special education for the less intelligent person. Similarly, apprenticeship is not seen as a worthwhile sacrifice. Because of the high failure rate of black apprentices, unions and contractors develop or retain the lazy, irresponsible stereotypes of the past. Both point out that despite the hardship of night classes for a period of two to five years, the training, like college, is an investment for the future. Blacks feel that the contractors do not understand that a career-minded minority cannot commit himself to the lengthy hardship of an apprenticeship when at any time he may be laid off or otherwise forced to terminate his apprenticeship. The risks in construction perceived by white and black apprentices are quite different.

An additional barrier to increased minority employment in construction is the inferior education of the inner city dweller. Many applicants who desire to enter the trades are frustrated by an inability to cope with math and other technical concepts which are standard fare in suburban schools.

Throughout the community we could find no great enthusiasm for any particular training program or for the Washington Plan itself. Community leaders are wary of Project BUILD, the union sponsored preapprenticeship program, because of its union orientation. BUILD, it is felt, focuses only on the apprentice route to entry and does not guarantee full union membership until apprenticeship is completed. Many in the community are distrustful of BUILD because of its poor retention record. A number of community leaders are on BUILD's Board of Directors, but there is not much organized community involvement. Project BUILD has strengthened its community contacts for recruiting purposes, but no firm ties exist as yet.

Despite the government's involvement on behalf of minorities, the unions are still deemed the primary barriers to equal employment opportunity. The use of permits, apprenticeship, and preapprenticeship status are seen as union devices to avoid giving minorities the long-term benefits of membership. Apprenticeship is viewed by those who have little contact with the industry as a black-only entry route. These attitudes appear virtually unchanged by events since the imposition of the Washington Plan. The community knows only that the Plan imposes requirements on the contractor and not directly on the union. In the absence of much public information about the Plan, they feel that the government has taken a politically easy road to compliance to avoid putting pressure on the unions. The average citizen believes that unions are untouched by the Plan; therefore, little progress should be expected.

Community leaders who were directly involved in the Washington Plan controversy from the outset are still highly critical of the SMSA orientation of the Plan. The low goals on construction sites in the District do not reflect the predominance of minority labor already living in the city. Minorities often will not respond to job opportunities created by the Washington Plan because the work sites may be in the hard-to-reach suburbs.

The concept of good faith effort is almost universally held as the prime loophole in compliance. The community lacks an understanding of the tests for good faith. It is felt that goals in the recalcitrant trades are too low, and that good faith requirements do not place enough pressure on unions. Therefore, many believe, unions are left free to maintain the status quo.

Because of the publicity surrounding the initial announcement and imposition of the Plan, community expectations of results have continually escalated. Many hear of compliance but see few new jobs for minorities. Their perceptions are not far from what we have found after months of study. There is little if any public exposure by government agencies of contractors found to be out of compliance. No contractor has ever been barred from further government work because of his failure to meet Washington Plan goals. Thus, minorities are not encouraged by the existence of a new regulation when, like others in the past, the penalties for non-compliance do not seem serious. After a seventeen-month study, the United States Commission on Civil Rights reported that since the issuance of E.O. 11246 "it was not until May 24, 1968 that the first notices of debarment were sent to contractors." It was further noted that "at that time there had not been a single cancellation or termination because of a contractor's discriminatory policies. In many cases public exposure was the only vehicle which seemed to bring about even minimal compliance." [79] Although we have seen that show cause hearings themselves are often effective in forcing contractor compliance, the community, in general, has not been aware of such efforts by the government.

The community has been looking for signs that the Plan is being strictly enforced. Some want to know the contrary, that the Plan is not working, in order to marshal community support for more militant action against the industry; but in the absence of publicized evidence of the performance of the Plan, community action appears neutralized.

In effect, the Plan has pacified all but the most militant. Because of the lack of cohesiveness in the community, what little unity the Washington Area Construction Industry Task Force achieved has dissipated. Pressure tactics and the resultant publicity have waned. Furthermore, some newspaper accounts imply that the Washington Plan will be a breakthrough for the minority worker. In this environment of cynicism among those close to the issue and conflicting reports as to the Plan's success, there can be little broad-based support for further militant action.

The OFCC bears the brunt of the activists' criticism. OFCC is seen as either unwilling or unable to vigorously enforce the Plan. In that the only formal contact between the community and the government occurs during quarterly Washington Plan Review Committee meetings, sponsored by OFCC, this agency is held accountable for the lack of debarments and responsible for stricter enforcement. Although both OFCC and community leaders seek the same goal, there is not a considerable amount of cooperation. Some see OFCC as the villain, because the Plan prevents more community action. OFCC, it is believed, is constrained politically

---

[79] *Construction Labor Report*, No. 787, October 21, 1970, pp. A2-3.

from winning the long-term gains for minorities that are needed. It is maintained that, like Project BUILD, the Plan is a pacifier which has government support and a degree of acceptance by the industry. The community interests are what are not served. While we find many of these criticisms overdone, we can understand how these views develop. Without sufficient understanding of OFCC's activities and more public evidence of enforcement, the average citizen can easily be led to believe that the Plan is accomplishing little or nothing.

We have found continued, albeit fragmented, efforts by community organizations to get more minorities into the construction industry. Furthermore, liberal union leaders, contractors, black union members, and many officials of the District government have been instrumental in lowering entry barriers. The Plan has not appreciably slowed their efforts, for most do not see the Plan as a cure-all. We believe that some of the progress, sometimes attributed to the Washington Plan, would have occurred without government involvement in 1970. Most community organizations report some increased interest in their minority referral capabilities. Contractors and unions are searching for informal sources of minority manpower.

In sum, community leaders believe that union membership for minorities is the only worthwhile goal. Membership offers an opportunity for high pay, security, benefits, escape from the ghetto, and invaluable work experience. Contractors, however, will not act on behalf of minorities to put pressure on the unions without extraordinary enforcement of the Plan by the government. Contractors will always fear losing whites, suffering union-led slowdowns, or destructive racial tension. The Plan is viewed only as a small step, not a solution.

A New Coalition

The community has not been totally silent on the issue of participation in Washington construction. There appears to be a new wave of activism focusing on the related problems of the minority contractors. The drafters of the Plan felt that increased employment of minority subcontractors would bring more minorities into the construction industry. The Washington Plan, many blacks point out, contains no mechanisms, incentives, or regulations to increase the amount of federal work done by minority contractors.

Again the METRO system has been the symbolic target. Many of those bringing attention to the underemployment of minorities on METRO sites in 1970 are now organizing new attacks on the underutilization of minority contractors. Minority contractors' groups, community leaders, and others have formed the METRO Coalition of Concerned Citizens. The old Washington Area Construction Industry Task Force is inactive, but several of its members are working in the new coalition. The coalition wants to win more contracts for minority firms by having such contracts either deliberately set aside or directly awarded to the subcontractor, not to the general contractors. As in the past, large general firms use a few subcontractors over and over rather than actively seek new firms. Since many of the METRO firms are based outside Washington, some of the work will go to firms and employees from out of town. The coalition, however, maintains that work in the District should go to District residents. Black contractors and trucking firms have won contracts for METRO work, but not enough, according to the coalition, which wants participation to be on a par with the levels of the Washington Plan.

Few community leaders believe that there are a sufficient number of experienced minority contractors equipped to tackle immediately a large share of METRO construction. They realize, however, that the lack of experience is, in the main, attributable to exclusion from lucrative federal contracts over the years and the vicious bonding circle that still exists. All contractors must obtain bonding certificates but minority contractors lack the necessary experience to fulfill bonding requirements. Affirmative action, which includes technical assistance, joint ventures with experienced firms, and other factors, is believed to be the only way to enable minority firms to join the mainstream of construction competition. Mere equal opportunity based on experience is not enough, for that will perpetuate the exclusion of the past. A small minority firm cannot gain experience in new construction techniques without contracts.

The coalition hopes to win 25 percent of all METRO contracts for minority contractors. It expects considerable resistance and legal objections to the concept of setting aside contracts, but it is looking into the feasibility of incorporating the minority contractor issue into the Washington Plan.

As expected, such action has brought criticism from white contractors who have long lived with competitive bidding. Many agree that minority firms should be given an equal opportunity to bid on METRO contracts, but set-asides are another matter. It will eventually be put to the government to decide whether affirmative action on behalf of minority firms will be needed to break the lack-of-experience circle and repay years of noncompetitive exclusion.

We believe that these events will bring attention to the problem of the minority contractor. The Washington Plan will be affected as the increased employment of minority subcontractors will increase a general contractor's ability to comply with Plan goals. We wonder, however, whether this new form of compliance will help achieve the ultimate objective of the Washington Plan of bringing more minorities into the skilled trades. Although winning large contracts will force many minority firms to expand their labor forces, the number of new minorities entering the industry in this manner will be less than the man-hour statistics eventually reported to federal agencies. Furthermore, one should not expect minority firms to immediately hire unemployed minorities to add to their work force. Once a marginal firm obtains a contract, it will be unable to provide the training or incur the costs of excess trainees that more profitable contractors have been able to do. This suggests an even larger financial commitment by the government, which may have to underwrite training costs. Otherwise, only existing black construction workers and even white craftsmen will, of necessity, be employed.

We believe, of course, that the focus on the minority contractor is a significant new development. The presence of more minority contracting firms on federal sites will, in the long run, help achieve what the Plan hopes to achieve. Minority firms will begin to grow and become self-sustaining. Successful bidding on later contracts will expand the hiring and training ability of minority firms. The older, more established firms will find that the positive aspects of this situation include a reduction of compliance pressures from escalating Washington Plan goals.

Perhaps because of the perceived limited impact of the Plan on the community, various organizations are beginning to seek new ways to penetrate the industry. Public interest lawyers have been working on legal action against discriminating unions and contractors. The suit against the bricklayers' local is one of the several expected to be filed throughout the life of the Washington Plan. Title VII suits will be the primary means for winning redress of racial discrimination charges in hiring and referral. Legal action will probably bring investigation of union hiring and testing practices and furthermore, small contractors, who are not covered by the Plan, will likely be charged with exclusionary practices.

Community organizations will continue the attempt to find new training and referral programs either with or without the co-operation of labor and the industry. Vocational training, offered at predominantly black schools, will be the focus of the Urban League and others.

In conclusion, we find little to indicate a great deal of confidence on the part of the community in the Washington Plan. The Plan will soon be half-completed, and community leaders claim that few minorities are as yet actually getting into the unions. Many critics who admit that the Plan has brought some progress will say that the Plan did not go far enough. Although the Plan is in their interest, they know too little of the results to change their basic distrust of government-sponsored plans.

We have witnessed progress and believe that contractors and unions do see that the times are changing. Decades of exclusion cannot be ended in only four years, but community impatience should surprise no one. Expectations of the Plan far exceed what will be realized. We do hope, on the other hand, that more information and more cooperation between the government and community will bring the understanding that is obviously needed.

If a change in Washington Plan requirements is not made, we fear that those minorities who have gained employment because of the Plan will vanish from the job sites at the Plan's termination. As our data indicate, blacks have gained in employment over the first year of the Plan, but they have not gained in union membership. Most of the new entrants are apprentices who face a long road ahead toward union membership.

INDUSTRY

The Washington Plan exerts varying degrees of pressure on different segments of the construction industry. The impact of the Plan on various groups and the reactions of these groups to the Plan are discussed below.

Contractor Associations

In general, contractor associations have taken a positive approach toward the Washington Plan. They appear to be making continued efforts at assisting their members in complying with the Plan's requirements. In fact, association leaders have always participated in discussions with the government and regularly attend meetings of the Washington Plan Review Committee. We have found, however, that representatives of the construction industry are highly critical of the Plan but are willing to continue a dialogue with community leaders and the government in order to meet the requirements of the Plan.

Union Contractors

Union contractors are bound by collective bargaining agreements to employ union referrals unless none are made available after a specified period of time has passed. Although OFCC maintains that the lack of minorities in the union is no excuse for noncompliance with Washington Plan standards, we have seen few contractors who would hire minorities without some union approval. There is no question that, faced with meeting goals, contractors are asking their unions for minority workers. What happens when none is available is another matter. Some contractors do advertise and hire minorities directly but others merely make attempts at finding minority candidates, then rely on proving a good faith effort in order to avoid debarment. Fearing slowdowns, a future of noncooperation from the union, or actual strikes, no contractors, especially those in the small firms, feel comforted by OFCC's promise to prosecute vigorously any union which takes such action. In addition, only the large general contractors possess the resources to recruit and absorb less skilled minority recruits.

Not all contractors, however, believe that the unions would thwart the direct hiring of minorities. Some unions would give membership to the new hires but many others would merely issue work permits, a common practice. The new minority is allowed to work, to contribute man-hours, but not to win full membership rights. Thus, when the job is completed, the union can shrink the work force by referring only members to the available work. Permit holders acquire no rights to future work. In fact, we have found cases where permit holders must endure a strike while card-carrying union members are referred to other bargaining jurisdictions for employment during the strike period. Contractors are virtually helpless to prevent such maneuvering.

The reliance upon referral unions, the fear of job actions, and union use of work permits may make it difficult for the contractor to employ blacks on a long-term basis. Minorities have gained construction jobs during the life of the Plan, but their job tenure is insecure. In addition, it is most probable that the lack of security has kept qualified minorities from presenting themselves for employment. As noted earlier, our research reveals that the Washington Plan has created a demand for minorities, but it often attracts the unemployed, unskilled, or hard core who are doomed to failure in a hard working, technical industry.

The Washington Plan has also not measurably increased the movement of minority laborers into the more skilled trades. In the nonunion sector, where contractors are free to assign workers at their own discretion, it is more likely that upgrading has occurred. In the union shop, craft lines restrict the free upgrading of predominantly black laborers. All contractors agree that the laborers offer a source of minorities who are already familiar with construction and willing to do the hardest work. The Washington Plan envisioned the laborers' ranks as a potential source of minorities to meet Plan requirements in the skilled trades. We have found signs of only marginal movement and we cannot say that the Plan has been the cause. Many laborers are unwilling, even when offered, to take a temporary cut in pay (to apprentice wages) in order to begin training for a new skill. Furthermore, attempts by the community to ally with laborer and trowel trades have largely failed.

There is little doubt that contractors perceive the requirements of the Washington Plan to be the meeting of percentage goals or the use of the "good faith" safety valve. Escalating goals pose serious problems for contractors employing the electro-mechanical trades. Plumbing contractors are unable to hire new workers while there is a high degree of unemployment in the trade. Furthermore, many small, all-white subcontractors have had a fixed work force for years. Hiring a minority to meet the Plan's goals may mean increasing their work force by 25 percent.

One contractor noted in an interview that "if contractors could not even bid without meeting the Plan's goals, there would be no bidding on government work." Although somewhat exaggerated, this man expressed the view of contractors who "promise now and worry about compliance later." He also points out that many in the industry are convinced that their good faith efforts are sufficient to avoid debarment.

Contractors are almost totally unaware of how their industry has performed under the Plan. While held in compliance on their own federal work, they do not feel part of an industry-wide effort to upgrade minorities. Reports from the Washington Plan Review Committee are found to be unsubstantial, when communicated to them at all. Most admit surprise when the percentage figures presented at those meetings are publicized. Electrical contractors, for example, admit in interviews that the percentage figures for their trade exceed the true participation of minorities in their trade. A more detailed discussion of the Washington Plan Review Committee reports will be given below.

One area of particular interest in our study has been the elevator installation business. This all-union segment of the industry has been tremendously affected by the Washington Plan as the trade has been virtually all-white for years. Now, with the requirements of the Washington Plan forcing a new hiring policy, elevator contractors are experiencing great difficulty in complying with the Plan. Because of the highly skilled nature of the work required, the contractors and unions are unable to quickly find new applicants who are qualified.

General contractors verify the difficulties of compliance in this trade. One claims that he will have to increase his bids substantially in order to have untrained minority elevator constructors present on the site. Another, who was unable to comply with the Plan's goals for this trade, lost a lucrative contract on METRO because his elevator subcontractor was unable to supply the requisite minority man-hours.

The major elevator contractors in Washington were interviewed. While one has avoided debarment by promising to hire one black for each white employed, there is no immediate prospect for a vast increase in jobs for minorities. In that there is no source of non-union mechanics experienced in this trade, those few blacks and other minorities hired to help meet the Plan's goals are put into helper categories if they pass a six-month probationary period.

At the time of our survey, two of the major elevator firms reported that their work force comprised only 4 percent and 6.8 percent minority. They admitted that they made a special effort to ensure that the minorities were always working, although whites had been laid off due to work slowdowns.

Contacts with Project BUILD, OIC, NAACP, Urban League, and vocational schools have increased as contractors are responding to Washington Plan pressures. Project BUILD in particular has offered to provide new applicants when work is available but it is probable that this trade will have severe compliance difficulty throughout the life of the Plan.

In summary, union contractors are well aware of the requirements and purposes of the Washington Plan and concur with the need to increase the number of minorities in construction. Under the pressure of compliance deadlines, contractors have taken affirmative steps to achieve their goals. Exceptions certainly exist, but contractors admit that the Plan provides a painful but necessary incentive to them and the unions to make special efforts to hire minorities.

Nonunion Contractors

Although many of the arguments arising out of the Washington Plan confirm the key role of the union in controlling entry into the trades, little attention has been focused on the nonunion sector. In fact, throughout the hearings and subsequent administration of the Washington Plan, people have taken on faith the civil rights record of nonunion industry. During the April 1970 hearings, there was little data presented about this sector and the Washington Plan Review Committee does not have one representative of non-union contractors.

In order to ascertain what the situation was in the Washington SMSA, a questionaire was circulated among nonunion contractors with the assistance of the Washington chapter, Associated Builders and Contractors, Inc. (ABC). Only thirty-three replied (about 15 percent) and it is likely that these had as good, or perhaps, a better racial employment balance than the average, since they were willing to submit data. Unfortunately, the data submitted were not similar in format to that presented in Chapter V. For this reason, these data are presented separately in Table 25. It should be noted that ABC membership includes both general contractors and subcontractors and those who answered the questionaire were a combination of all types.

TABLE 25. *Washington Plan*
Minority Participation in Nonunion Construction
Washington SMSA

Trades	Percentage of Minority Employees			
	Supervisors	Skilled	Unskilled	Total
Electrical	0.0	3.0	75.0	6.7
Mechanical	0.0	7.1	39.0	14.4
Carpentry	13.8	41.4	48.0	41.3
Trowel	46.2	67.7	69.5	67.5
Laborers [a]	5.0	15.4	87.5	46.1

Source: Questionaire circulated by authors.

[a] The different skill levels for laborers is attributable to laborers performing various duties for nonunion contractors while remaining classified as laborers.

The percentage of minorities throughout the sample work force was 26.1 percent, almost exactly the proportion of minorities in the Washington SMSA. We were most interested, however, in seeing if there was a difference between the nonunion and union sector in the concentration of minorities in particular trade categories. History and our study reveal that the electromechanical trades in the union sector were most exclusionary and that blacks were concentrated in the trowel trades. One would hypothesize that without union barriers, the proportion of minorities in the skilled trades would be higher than it presently is in the union sector. Our sample, though hardly conclusive, does not support that hypothesis. In fact, it suggests that there is little difference between sectors. Minority concentrations in the lower skill categories may be primarily due to educational and training inadequacies in the community at large. Based upon the data in Table 25 and our field interviews, we believe that the average nonunion contractor is nonexclusionary and indeed wants quality work for the wages he pays. Unlike his union counterpart, the open-shop contractor pays little attention to specific hiring requirements for minorities and actually has made much less effort to recruit in the minority community. Simply put, he too hires those who come in to apply, regardless of race, but has yet to become involved in any extensive affirmative action. He is generally uninformed about the Washington Plan and is more willing to object publicly to the "unreasonable" intrusion of the government into his own hiring responsibilities. Many nonunion contractors have always hired minorities, but as in the union sector, blacks are rare in the electrical, mechanical, and plumbing trades.

Actually, only 10 percent of ABC members do government work and many of these work on projects valued at less than $500,000, primarily on military bases, schools, hospitals, or renovations. Interestingly, those with government contracts often use union subcontractors, if they submit the lowest bid. Because of the requirement to pay (higher) Davis-Bacon wages on federal projects, many open-shop subcontractors are reluctant to bid on government jobs where they would have to pay the higher rates. Employees may join the union after growing accustomed to the higher standard of living.

The ABC has had a formal apprenticeship program for five years and there are approximately 125 apprentices in the organization now. The percentage of minorities in the program varies frequently. The ABC suffered a drop from 26 percent to 19 percent minority during a one-month period, and is now trying to get Manpower Administration funding for a small, high-skill, all-minority training program for fifty people. This program would provide disadvantaged minorities with the skills necessary to enter nonunion apprenticeship in plumbing, carpentry, sheet metal, and electrical work. Starting compensation for the thirty-week program would be $2.75 per hour.

All past efforts to recruit apprentices, however, have not been successful. Many applicants refuse to travel to the suburbs for work. As for work in the District, it has been noted that advertised openings do not result in a stampede to the job. So far, the most successful source of applicants has been the Apprentice Information Center (AIC), where referrals are closely coordinated.

Other training is provided in federal sites where the Davis-Bacon Act requires training slots. Since money is available to pay apprentices at 45 percent of full wage, contractors are able to hire laborers for less than laborer's wages by designating them apprentices. These men do receive some on-the-job training.

Foster states that "the *primary* means of skill acquisition is training, formal and informal, within the construction industry itself." [80] Foster also indicates that many construction craftsmen received other than apprenticeship training. Especially noted was on-the-job training received in the nonunion sector.[81] If this is universal, it may be that the emphasis on apprenticeship training for new minorities as practiced in Washington will delay the realization of the Plan's objectives.

Like their union counterparts, only the small subcontractors employ the trades covered by the plan and many employ only a handful of employees, most of whom are white. One subcontractor interviewed expressed the typical problems which would arise under a Washington Plan contract: of his eleven employees, only one, the latest hired, is black. The Plan would require a minority proportion far in excess of this for his trade. He could never comply without firing a white employee. In fact, a slow-down of work may dictate the layoff of at least one employee. He admits that he may discharge a white in order to keep the

---

[80] Howard G. Foster, "Nonapprentice Sources of Training in Construction," *Monthly Labor Review*, Vol. 93, No. 2, February 1970, p. 26 (emphasis in original).

[81] *Ibid.*, p. 21.

black on his work force, despite the violation of seniority rules and fairness.

Nonunion contractors show an even weaker communication link with community organizations than do union firms. While several are now advertising in the black media and submitting requests for minority applicants with the ABC, most have no informal ties with minority organizations. In fact, nonunion contractors express surprise over learning the extent of union construction firms' efforts to recruit, train, and retain minorities.

Those nonunion contractors covered by the Plan demonstrated unexpected candor in pointing out weaknesses in the compliance system. As in the union sector, most contractors sign the contracts and worry about compliance later. One said that the Plan "is being met on the forms;" another said that the Plan "functions in the contractor's office."

Although it is not a widespread practice, there are instances of contractors shifting workers, rather than hiring new ones, to meet compliance requirements. In one case, a union subcontractor for a nonunion general contractor was required to increase the man-hours done by minority sheet metal workers. When the union failed to provide the men, the subcontractor paid other minority employees sheet-metal wages rather than hire men off the street. He won compliance without hiring a single new minority. In another incident a mechanical contractor was threatened with debarment. Because the general contractor reports only this subcontractor's man-hours on the federal project, the subcontractor was able to shift minorities from his private site and comply with the Plan. Again, no new minorities were hired.

While actual compliance has not yet proven a great difficulty in the nonunion sector, the Washington Plan has brought the problem of low minority participation in the industry to the attention of government contract seekers. Our findings, however, indicate a less-than-deep involvement in the upgrading and recruiting of minorities. We found no evidence of outright racism; nevertheless, the prevailing attitude focuses on equal rights, rather than affirmative action. The drafters of the Washington Plan believe that mere equal treatment will not end the minority's outsider status in construction. Affirmative action and extra effort are seen as necessary to compensate for years of poor education, lack of experience, and discrimination. We believe that the lack of government involvement in the open sector explains the difference in attention to equal employment problems. The union sector, ironically, seems more involved in affirmative action. Increased union involvement in equal employment matters indicates an additional value of the Washington Plan.

Minority Contractors

Minority contractors share many of the same problems faced by their white counterparts. In order to compete, they must find qualified minority workers. Although major white contractors have hired unskilled trainees, despite the obvious costs, in order to comply with the Plan, few minority contractors can be so generous. Ironically, the marginal minority contractor is even more demanding when it comes to hiring. In fact, we have found signs that minority contractors will hire skilled whites, or seek white referrals from the union, in order to compete effectively. One successful minority contractor has been accused of "becoming economically white." In addition, minority contractors lack the resources to provide adequate training for minority employees. Thus, minorities entering the industry through this route may remain at the lower end of the skill spectrum.

Minorities have recently organized a black contractors' association, The Washington Area Contractors Association. WACA has approximately 100 members, and, in the first four months of its existence, won $1,676,632 in construction work. Unfortunately, most of the member firms are small and will never have the capacity to do work on large federal sites covered by the Washington Plan.

The establishment of a minority contractors' association, however, is a significant step. With the demand for minority workers generated by the Plan, vigorous community efforts, and the encouragement by federal agencies, there should be increased attention focused on the minority contractor. We have seen cases of successful bidding by black subcontractors, despite lower bids from other subcontractors. With the existing equal employment and Plan requirements, minority contractors have been given a boost because of their singular ability to meet compliance standards. White contractors have complained about this seemingly preferential treatment, but are also seeking the good minority firms for joint ventures.

Minority firms have also been used in an occasional costly scheme to provide minority man-hours to meet Plan requirements.

Subcontracting low-skill and petty work to a small minority contractor puts minorities on the payroll for reporting purposes, yet provides no new employment.

Only 5 of the 100 members in WACA are union contractors; therefore, few minorities have won membership into the union through this route. Those who are union members, however, may be referred to white contractors for work in order to meet the goals of the Plan.

In sum, minority contractors should become a more frequently employed source of minority labor on federal projects because of the Plan. It is doubtful, however, that by the last year of the Plan, any sizable number of new minorities will enter the industry through this route. Existing minority contractors and their employees may move from a commercial site to a federal site, but until minority contractors are awarded contracts large enough to encourage their hiring extensively in the community, progress will be slow. Furthermore, those minority firms whose members do not participate in union training or apprentice programs will lag behind their unionized counterparts in skills.

Unions

In most construction trades, the union utilizes an exclusive hiring hall arrangement whereby employment and referral-to-work decisions are made by the union, not the employer. There is good reason for this arrangement: construction requires many skilled trades, some of which may only be needed for a matter of days on any one particular site. Unlike laborers, cement finishers, or engineers, for example, electrical or sheet metal workers are not needed throughout the life of the project. Thus, the contractor merely calls the union for craftsmen at the appropriate time. Exceptions certainly exist, but in the skilled trades covered by the Washington Plan the union has firm control over entry and employment.

Unions have always been exclusionary, but not only for racist reasons. Attempts to limit the availability of skilled workers, thereby creating an artificial scarcity, and to reserve membership for friends and relatives, are also significant factors. The potential pool of minorities poses an economic threat to unions in Washington. But although affirmative action plans are not welcomed by organized labor, they have supported apprentice outreach programs.

One cannot say that there are few minorities on construction sites; a cursory tour of Washington construction projects will disprove that notion. Union leaders often cite statistics which demonstrate that the proportion of minorities in construction exceeds their representation in the population. However, the statistics do not point out the continued concentration of minorities in the lowest skill trades.

The AFL-CIO is quick to defend itself against allegations of exclusion, pointing out that over 5,000 minorities were brought into construction between 1966 and 1969 through apprentice outreach programs. Furthermore, while all apprentices increased 38.6 percent from 1950 to 1969, minority apprentices increased 364.7 percent.[82] Most of the increases, however, were made in largely black, lower paying trades.

Although government action to increase participation in the construction trades has been primarily limited to legal/legislative action, the Philadelphia Plan marked a new attempt to bring pressure on organized labor. The approach was indirect. Union contractors facing debarment because of their failure to meet Plan goals would either hire minorities on their own or transfer the pressure to the union. Unions, it was believed, would not be able to resist compliance because either they would lose complete control over entry, or their members would be unemployed because of the debarment of a union contractor.

Although unions are not actually bound by the Plan, their actions in response to the demand for minorities created by the Washington Plan are most important. Contractors have hired minorities to meet Plan goals, but the mere increase of man-hours performed by minorities does not guarantee increased long-term opportunity. Apprenticeship, permits to work, and trainee status can always be terminated. As stated in Chapter V, many of the man-hours reported as work performed by minorities are accomplished by men who are already in the industry. New entries, if on permit or given less than full membership rights, may become only temporary participants in construction. Once each project is completed, those hired on permit are not assured of any further work. Such employment rights go only to union members.

Unions have almost universally perceived affirmative action plans as quota systems and have vigorously opposed their implementation.

---

[82] *Construction Labor Report*, February 17, 1971, No. 804, p. A13.

C. J. Haggerty, President of the Construction and Building Trades Department of the AFL-CIO stated in 1969 that "we are 100 percent opposed to a quota system, whether it be called the Philadelphia Plan or whatever." [83] Louis Sherman, General Counsel for the AFL-CIO says that "a range of percentages which, if you read it, makes it entirely clear that what is intended is a quota system . . . even if the employer engages in so-called good faith compliance, it is a quota system. The point is that the race factor, which is not supposed to be taken into account under the law, must be taken into account." [84]

Many people in organized labor view affirmative action plans as handouts to those unwilling to go "the hard way." Exclusionary institutions are rarely mentioned, but the case of the unqualified minority who received a special break is often cited. Unions have focused special attention on apprenticeship, as increased minority participation seems inevitable. While apprenticeship most likely does provide long-range educational benefits, a very large percentage of journeymen in most trades never went through full apprenticeship. The emphasis on the apprentice route of entry is not as racially motivated as most critics think, however; in the highly skilled trades, where technology is rapidly advancing, apprenticeship is becoming a must for white and black. Furthermore, and perhaps most importantly, most minorities now applying for membership in the unions are young and inexperienced. Thus, lateral entry or direct classification as journeyman is unlikely. The community remains doubtful of these reasons and claims that apprenticeship is a black-only entry route. This controversy demands further study.

Although less prevalent than a decade ago, nepotism is still a barrier to minority entry into the trades. Union leaders still make special efforts to find a place for relatives in the union, but are, ironically, often frustrated when these individuals seek other careers. The father-to-son tradition is waning as construction is looked upon as dirty work and white collar careers became more attractive. One business agent pointed out that his son's desire to go to college is the price of his achievement of middle class status. The "hard hat" image and the prestige of the white collar job have also affected the minority youth, who has not responded to increased advertising in the construction industry.

---

[83] *New York Times*, September 24, 1969.

[84] Francis T. Coleman, "The Philadelphia Plan Goes to Washington," *American Bar Association Journal*, Vol. 57, February 1971, p. 139.

Washington unions, like their contractors, report that the major bar to increased minority employment is the low skill level of the majority of new applicants. The unions steadfastly adhere to their position that standards must be maintained. Several unions, however, have consciously lowered their entry standards in order to let in marginal applicants. In many cases, they admit that the Washington Plan has forced this action. In addition, many unions have reacted to increased attention to minority hiring by creating their own equal employment positions. They have found that an apprenticeship coordinator, especially if black, will improve recruiting and reduce dropout rates in apprenticeship.

Many labor leaders are cooperating with industry and the community to end the years of minority exclusion. While constrained by their position in public, many of those interviewed indicated that progress would be made, although at a considerably slower pace than the Plan envisioned. Our survey of organized labor reveals a broad spectrum of attitudes, ranging from this progressive outlook to token integration and to continued resistance. In general, those who welcome minorities include the ones affected by the Washington Plan, with the recalcitrant trades responding slowly to government pressure. Unfortunately, we have not found a breakthrough in all of the eleven covered trades, and we seriously doubt that union membership will show a dramatic change by the end of the Plan.

Business agents admit that unions are now making special efforts to attract minorities. The costs, however, have been a raising of racial tensions and a high turnover rate. Marginally qualified workers will be laid off and many of the hard core applicants are likely to drop out. While most agree that the unions have waited too long to integrate, they do not believe that the percentage goal system will be successful. Although mere employment by a trade does not necessarily qualify one for union membership, qualified workers cannot become union members without first being employed. Thus, the hiring of qualified minorities often dictates progress toward increasing the number of minorities in the union. The Carpenters' collective bargaining agreement with the Construction Contractors Council, for example, states that "it shall also be a condition of employment that all employees covered by this agreement who are hired on or after its execution date shall, on and after the seventh (7th) day following the beginning of such employment, become and remain members of the union." Employment must come first.

Project BUILD

Almost every union, most contractors, and a lesser number of community leaders have had some contact with Project BUILD. We have accumulated much information about this training program, but will restrict our observations to those pertinent to the Washington Plan.

Project BUILD is a union-sponsored craft training program established by the Greater Washington Central Labor Council, AFL-CIO, and the Manpower Administration of the United States Department of Labor. The Washington Building and Construction Trades Council is a cooperating agency. BUILD received its first funding of $416,000 in January 1968 and has been continually refunded since. Initially designed to train and prepare hard-core minorities for apprenticeship, BUILD has now developed a skill refinement program for potential lateral entries into the construction trades.

Project BUILD has always been a controversial program. Initially, attempts to quicky prepare poorly educated unemployed resulted in a high dropout rate among graduating preapprentices. Throughout our field work we have heard strong criticism of BUILD graduates who were referred to work but subsequently quit, were arrested, or lacked the necessary motivation to be retained. Many union leaders and contractors resist closer contact with BUILD because of past experiences.

The dropout rate of BUILD graduates was most heavy during the first classes. The Director of Project BUILD claimed during the April 1970 hearings that 27.5 percent of the 141 graduates of BUILD's first two cycles (classes) had dropped out of apprenticeship in the first year. An independent investigation revealed that of a sample of 88 BUILD graduates listed as apprentices, 56 were not registered with the D.C. Apprenticeship Council within six months of graduation.[85] The poor quality of applicants, inadequate training, and resistance by unions and employers all account for the high failure rate. Our survey, however, indicates that both the retention rate and employer union acceptance rate of the BUILD graduate have improved and are now in line with industry experience.

According to Project BUILD, a total of 249 minority apprentices had entered construction prior to the imposition of the Washington

---

[85] Information obtained by an impartial investigation by a government official whose name must be held in confidence.

Plan. Since then, improved followup services have diminished the dropout rate.

A key factor in Project BUILD's prominence in Washington is its acceptance by organized labor. Despite its all-minority nature, BUILD is solidly union oriented. Dissatisfaction with its graduates has been caused primarily by their high failure rate. Project BUILD is now a comprehensive training program which includes extensive counseling, along with skill training. BUILD staff members strive to keep in touch with graduates to ensure that they are still on the job.

The Craftsman Refinement Center has had more favorable reviews in the industry. Former nonunion employees or those with prior related experience are given upgrading assistance. It is hoped that these graduates will win direct journeyman's status. Under the current contract, BUILD intends to recruit, train, and place 200 of these advanced trainees.

For all of its weakness, Project BUILD offers a well-advertised, union-sponsored minority manpower program which will continue to be a primary source of minorities for unions and contractors forced to comply with the Washington Plan.

Project BUILD has conducted an extensive public relations campaign to inform contractors of its services. Recently, the Executive Director sent letters to contractors throughout the Washington area to inform them that Project BUILD was "able and willing to provide you with any number of trainees in any craft of the building and construction trades at any time." The letter noted that such aid would prove helpful to those required to comply with the Washington Plan. We believe that BUILD's offer exceeds its capabilities, but should go a long way in opening communication channels with suburban contractors who claim little contact with minority manpower sources. BUILD should be most successful in those Plan trades in which preapprentice training is provided: electrical, painting, plumbing, sheet metal, and steamfitting. In our survey, however, we have witnessed the referral of minorities to unions which do not provide instructors to BUILD. In this capacity BUILD acts essentially as a placement service. Remediation, counseling, and work-related training can, however, help prepare the applicant for the union's testing process.

Where traditional contact between the union and Project BUILD has been limited, BUILD has had less success in placing apprentices. Perhaps in the future, when a greater number of experienced minorities apply for BUILD programs, BUILD may increase its success in placing minorities in such trades as the glaziers, elevator constructors, ironworkers, tilesetters, lathers, boilermakers, and asbestos workers.

Spokesmen from BUILD indicate that they have felt both positive and negative effects from the Washington Plan. In one case, a contractor called for an apprentice because of Plan requirements. The man referred to that job reported that he had been allowed to work two hours a day for a short period and was then subjected to a layoff. On the positive side, the Plan has increased the number of enrollees and helped improve the rentention rate of BUILD graduates, for, because of the Plan, contractors are now more hesitant to lay off minorities.

Project BUILD has also become a vehicle for recruiting nonunion minority craftsmen for entry into organized labor. Again BUILD has had its difficulties. In a recent case, recruited and referred minorities were eventually laid off. Thus BUILD's status with unions is not universal.

In sum, Project BUILD remains rather controversial. Many criticize the high attrition rate of its graduates, the limited nature of its training resources, its union orientation, and its use of taxpayers' money. BUILD has caused rivalry with existing training programs. Some feel that Manpower funding of this program prevents the establishment of competing programs. Personal conflicts have affected the degree of cooperation between BUILD and the unions. The nature of the typical BUILD recruit, hard-core and unemployed, allegedly guarantees failure in a highly skilled trade, and thus old stereotypes are perpetuated. BUILD has taken attention away from existing employment services, such as the AIC, schools, and veterans' services. These and many other criticisms are voiced from all sides.

Project BUILD has become an unquestioned institution in the Washington construction industry and should expand its influence because of the Washington Plan. Although BUILD remains in contact with community organizations, it should be considered primarily a union program. It is doubtful that BUILD will ever work closely with such community organizations as the Urban League. Representatives of BUILD, on the other hand, should become more involved in the administration of the Washington Plan. The Executive Director should participate with other representatives from industry and labor at meetings of the Washington Plan Review Committee.

In evaluating the impact of the Washington Plan, we have found that Project BUILD has been affected, and that its success in bringing more minorities into the trades has been increased by the Plan. Conceived before the Plan, Project BUILD has slowly improved its services and established the industry, union, and community contacts necessary to make such a program effective. Project BUILD and other training programs are not replacements for the Plan, because they represent special interests. On the other hand, much of the progress achieved by the Washington Plan was due in part to efforts like Project BUILD.

GOVERNMENT

This section will examine the administration of the Plan, as well as seek answers to the following questions: What other programs have affected the Plan? How much cooperation exists between the government and industry, labor, or the community? How are the government's efforts received? What regulations exist to enforce equal employment in the industry? Can government regulation achieve success where voluntarism does not exist?

Compliance Administration

The capacity of the Office of Federal Contract Compliance to administer the Plan is severely limited by budgeting and staffing problems. OFCC has been expected to coordinate equal employment programs, monitor numerous construction plans, collect and distribute data, and develop affirmative action plan policy. Because it has a small central staff and a minimum of field personnel, there have been problems in carrying out such a wide range of duties.

As OFCC resources were further strained by the increased number of imposed and voluntary plans throughout the country, the role of OFCC shifted more toward coordination of compliance activities of federal agencies. Monitoring of plans has consisted more and more of the analysis of man-hour statistics as reported by contracting agencies. Direct OFCC involvement, of course, continues during the fact-finding hearings, plan development, and implementation phases, and OFCC offices throughout the country are assigned with overseeing local plan administration and compliance effectiveness within their region.

Because inconsistent compliance enforcement among agencies has been a persistent problem, OFCC has continually issued directives and otherwise attempted to simplify the compliance process. Compliance officials in governmental agencies have removed many of the defects in the compliance reporting system and contractors are becoming more familiar with the required reports.

Early in this study it was noted that a great deal of confusion existed as a result of varied interpretations of compliance requirements.

The compliance system under the Washington Plan is monitored primarily through man-hour reports and site inspections. When submitting bids on federal contracts, construction contractors must agree to meet the man-hour percentage goals incorporated into the Plan, for those crafts employed throughout the life of the contract. Successful contractors are required to submit monthly minority utilization reports (Form 66) to their contracting agencies. These reports must indicate the man-hours performed in all crafts (not just Plan trades) by race and the number of minorities employed during the month covered. Individual monthly reports are collected by contracting agencies and combined reports are sent to OFCC. Thus, OFCC maintains a data file which includes all man-hours performed by contractors on federally assisted or federally funded sites. Contractors are also required to include in their reports all work done by subcontractors and work done on private sites. By examining the total work force, it is believed, contractors will be unable to shift minorities from private sites to federal sites in order to gain compliance. It is in the private site reporting area, however, that the system partially breaks down.

In addition, since OFCC does not solicit data on union membership, the Plan does not distinguish effectively between union and nonunion contractors. Furthermore, the data collected do not indicate how many employees are working on temporary work permits.

The second phase of the compliance system is actual on-site inspection by agency compliance officials. On-site visits are held four times throughout each contract life. The first review is conducted when the project is 10 to 20 percent completed; other visits occur at 30 to 40 percent and 50 to 60 percent, and the last review is held when 70 to 75 percent of the work has been completed. Reviews include examination of employers' records and payroll data, interviews wtih minority employees, and a generally thorough fact-finding tour of the contractor's facilities. The rigorousness of this visit has in the past depended somewhat on the methods of the individual inspector, although explicit guidelines have now reduced this form of inconsistency.

The man-hour data are compiled quarterly for the preparation of a report to the Washington Plan Review Committee. This report indicates the percentage of man-hours performed by minorities in the Plan trades for each agency, as well as aggregate percentages.

The number, not names, of noncomplying and complying contractors is also given.

OFCC requires that contracting agencies insist that noncomplying contractors comply with the Plan or else begin debarment action. In noncompliance cases, hearings are held by each agency at which time contractors are required to show cause why they should not be found out of compliance. Contractors are given thirty days to meet the goals or demonstrate sufficient good faith effort to avoid debarment. No Washington contractor has been debarred to date. The cost to management and the embarrassment of show cause hearings in many cases are sufficient to force contractors into compliance. Contractors have admitted to our researchers that one show cause hearing is enough to make them want to avoid any further charges of noncompliance.

According to the Plan, hearings can be reopened to reevaluate the goal requirements for any particular trade. Such a renegotiation of goals, however, would set a risky and costly precedent. Contractors or unions appealing the goal ranges would have to be well prepared with facts. Obviously, some of the ranges have become unrealistic because of economic conditions in the particular trades, but there are not likely to be any appeals for modifying the ranges because unions and contractors do not even realize that they have such an opportunity and few are able to present sufficient supporting data. When the goals have become too high as a result of unemployment in a particular trade, contracting agencies have used good faith as a measure of compliance.

Since the goals were developed from statistics which were often only best estimates, projections of manpower needs, attrition, openings, and minority manpower availability are only forecasts whose precision will always be open to question. Experience in the trades after one year of the Plan, however, should have been sufficient to justify some reevaluation of the goals. The one-year point review of goal ranges provided for in the Plan was not held, to our knowledge, nor was it accomplished internally. We could find no union or industry representative who had been asked to contribute to this review.

OFCC Philosophy

The philosophy behind the Plan as expressed by OFCC is as follows: Once enough minorities have entered the industry because of the Plan, the government will be able to leave the industry alone. Once minorities are accepted by contractors and the unions, the jobs will open up. Other minorities will see more of their peers on work sites in the city and will apply. There should be a spreading effect as qualified minorities are lured from nonunion or related industries by the prospect of higher pay and benefits. The Plan provides the stick to serve as a substitute for a voluntary solution which would work only when the community is sufficiently well organized to deal directly with contractors and unions. The Washington Plan Review Committee, as discussed below, is seen as the best forum for the expression of community interests.

Our discussion below indicates that the Washington Plan Review Committee, and the Plan itself, have not brought change as fast as OFCC envisioned. The Plan is almost at the halfway point, but new employment opportunities for minorities are still limited.

On the positive side, regional OFCC officials have, in many cases, accomplished more than compliance enforcement. Individual regional directors have become involved in recruiting and placement problems and have assisted contractors' groups in locating community organizations which may be able to meet some of their minority manpower needs. The Philadelphia office's regional director has responsibility for both the Philadelphia and Washington Plans. Although he continues to plan Review Committee meetings and prepare the quarterly summaries for the Committee, we believe that he is overburdened. Because of his small staff, both plans cannot get the attention they need.

Washington Plan Review Committee

The most likely vehicle for an effective administration of the Plan is the Washington Plan Review Committee. In actuality, however, we have found the Review Committee operating far below its potential.

The Washington Plan Review Committee was designed by OFCC to provide a continuing forum for representatives of all parties involved with the Washington Plan. Representatives of labor, industry, local government, community, and OFCC would meet quarterly to discuss the progress of the Plan. Members of the committee include representatives of unions, contractors' associations, the mayor's office, the Washington Area Construction Industry Task Force, the Urban League, and others. Most of the participants were actively involved in the preimposition hearings and negotiations. The Director of OFCC convenes and informally chairs the committee meetings which are held in the Department of Labor Building.

At present, the Review Committee meeting is held quarterly as prescribed but lasts for little more than one hour and is poorly attended. No union official has participated in the last two meetings and at the most recent meeting (at the time of this writing), held on December 14, 1971, only five of the fourteen members were present. No representatives of the community participated. Few of those members who usually attend have confidence that the Committee meetings will be productive.

The typical meeting centers around the release of the Washington Plan status report, consisting of a memorandum from the Director of OFCC to the Review Committee which contains a summary of man-hours performed, by race, on each of the federal contracts that fall under the Washington Plan. This cumulative report is compiled from data received from the contracting agencies. Most members now perceive the Review Committee meetings as the opportunity to receive and discuss the quarterly reports. None expect to use the forum for coordinating and communicating their needs. Many see no value in attending.

One great failing of the Washington Plan is the absence of a visible measuring stick for all concerned to evaluate the results of the Plan. Although OFCC does not intend to use the quarterly reports as the sole indicator of the Plan's performance, the figures in these reports have become this indicator by default. In early reports, the overall percentage of man-hours performed by minorities in the crafts involved were taken as the measure of success or failure of the Plan. Members of the Committee and the general public would compare these percentages with the appropriate yearly goal requirements. Unfortunately, since each report in 1971 was prepared in a different format, many of the Committee members claimed that they were unable to understand them.

These overall percentages are on occasion, released to the press, and the public then uses the data as a measure of the Plan's progress. The Department of Labor, for example, released its findings based on these reports approximately one year after the imposition of the Plan. The release, which gained considerable publicity in Washington, claimed that "on the average, employment of minorities in construction trades covered by the Washington Plan is running within the ranges set when the minority-employment plan was implemented a year ago." [86] Percentage figures and the goal requirements for the first year were also given. Because no other evaluation of the Plan had been made, Committee

---

[86] U.S. Department of Labor, News Release, USDL 7-319, June 10, 1971.

members and the public assumed that the percentages given did in fact indicate that the Plan was succeeding in all but four trades.

Pressure on the unions becomes dependent on these reports. Publicized accounts in national periodicals noted that the "electrical workers, iron workers and elevator constructors are exceeding their required ranges. The painters and paperhangers, the plumbers, the steamfitters and sheet metal workers are within the ranges set. The lathers, with 8.3 percent of their workers, are below the range of 16 to 22 percent, and the elevator constructors [*sic*], tile and terrazzo workers and glaziers have employed no minorities." [87]

Committee members are further confused by the data used to make up these reports. The private work of contractors is not reported, but some amount of federal work below the $500,000 minimum is included. We do not know if contractors with more than one federal contract have their non-Plan federal work double-counted as they report all of their sites to each agency.

In some reports, percentages for each craft were computed. In another report only total man-hours were given. Thus, much time at one meeting was spent interpreting the report, not discussing other problems.

OFCC admits that some contracting agencies are not fully reporting all federal and private work. This, combined with the absence of an operational, computerized data collection system, has prevented OFCC from preparing a more precise and comprehensive report. It is apparent that without such a reporting system, contractors will continue to win compliance by ensuring that all minorities are on federal work sites. Contractors confirm that compliance officials still have a federal-site orientation and are only beginning to examine carefully a contractor's company-wide posture. If contractors and unions are indeed managing their minority resources, compliance becomes a matter of ensuring that existing minority employees are at work where it counts.

Compliance can be easy for even the most white-dominated trades in which very few man-hours are worked in a quarter. One craft went from 0 percent to 20.4 percent minority in one quarter, according to the quarterly report from OFCC. The elevator constructors, who were noted as being far out of compliance in June 1971, were able to meet their goals with room to spare in September by employing only 426 more minority man-

---

[87] *Daily Labor Report,* June 9, 1971, p. A-6.

hours; that could have been accomplished by employing one black for ten and one-half weeks! The tile and terrazzo workers went from 0 to 68.4 percent minority with only 828 additional minority man-hours, the equivalent of two minorities working less than ten and one-half weeks.

Bureau of Apprenticeship and Training

The Bureau of Apprenticeship and Training (BAT) has become increasingly involved in pressuring unions to take affirmative action in recruiting and training minorities. On April 8, 1971 the Department of Labor issued a revision of apprenticeship rules.[88] "The regulations call for the promotion of equality of opportunity in apprenticeship by requiring affirmative action and by coordinating the prohibitions with other equal opportunity programs. To provide affirmative action, sponsors of programs must follow a pattern of identification, positive recruitment, training and motivation of present and potential minority group apprentices."[89] The regulations require state apprenticeship agencies to ensure that registered apprenticeship programs take various affirmative action steps outlined in the regulations. The regulations also call for periodic auditing of the programs and other action by these agencies to ensure that equal employment is being practiced. Sufficient time had not elapsed at the time that this report was written to determine the extent to which this regulation might serve to increase minority apprenticeship participation. In addition, the D.C. Apprenticeship Council does not seem to have dramatically altered its procedures.

CONCLUSION

The Washington Plan has achieved success in increasing the share of blacks in skilled construction employment. It has not, as yet, assured that Negroes will become a permanent part of the work force through union membership. Meanwhile, the black community remains skeptical of progress, which in turn hinders progress, and the government agencies lack both the coordination and the funds necessary to perform the task allotted to them.

---

[88] Title 29, Part 30, "Equal Employment Opportunity in Apprenticeship and Training," *Federal Register*, Vol. 36, No. 68, April 8, 1971.

[89] *Daily Labor Report*, April 7, 1971, p. A-16.

PART III

Indianapolis, Indiana

CHAPTER VII

Negroes in Construction: The History in Indianapolis, Indiana

Indianapolis has traditionally been a border city in outlook and practice. Located within the territory of the Northwest Ordinance, which, as enacted in 1787, barred slavery within its confines, it has been peopled by a mixture of southern whites and blacks, European immigrants, and northern migrants. Indianapolis was a stronghold of the Ku Klux Klan in the 1920s, and enforced segregation was extended, strengthened, and remained in effect until the 1950s.

The position of the black craftsman in Indianapolis today can be better understood by examining the historical factors which have influenced his environment. The direct influences of education, politics, civil rights, economics, and union attitudes are examined in the following sections.

1800-1920

One of the earliest manifestations of racial disharmony in the North grew out of the question of whether to permit or forbid black children to go to public school. At the same time, competition between Negroes and whites over jobs and the question of Negro voting rights followed the migration of blacks from the South to the North. These issues became burning questions in Indiana and its capital city, Indianapolis.

Education

By the mid-1800s, the question of whether or not to provide schools for Negroes had surfaced in local politics. As late as 1847, no educational funds had been appropriated for Negroes; those who attended school did so through private means or, occasionally, were admitted to public schools if their districts did not share the prevailing prejudices.[90] The legislature considered the problem in 1855 and voted to exempt Negroes' property from taxes supporting Indiana schools.[91] This solution was harsher than the existing situation. Legal exclusion led to the development of private schools, most of which were church-affiliated, but there were still few families that could avail themselves of this alternative.[92]

In 1869, however, the state legislature again considered the question and reversed its earlier decision by passing legislation requiring schools for Negroes, even if it meant consolidating districts.[93] It was not until 1877 that laws permitting Negroes to attend white schools were adopted.[94] The 1877 legislation also gave local authorities the power to determine which type of system, joint or separate, was to be maintained. The results show that towns with large numbers of Negroes retained segregated facilities. Even where integrated facilities were maintained, the Negro was pressured, by economics, to leave school and find work when legally possible, usually at the age of fourteen.[95] As a result, few Negroes graduated from either type of school for many years.

Politics and Civil Rights

In the postwar struggle for Negro rights, several black political leaders emerged in the state, each advocating devout allegiance to the Republican party as gratitude for emancipation. However, their support of the GOP was so emphatic that they failed to use the party in their struggle for equality. Similarly, the party took for granted the Negro support and saw little need to share the rewards of victory with them. Black leaders and newspapers continually endorsed the party's candidates but

---

[90] Emma Lou Thornbrough, *The Negro in Indiana Before 1900* (Indianapolis: Indiana Historical Bureau, 1957), pp. 165-166.

[91] Richard G. Boone, *History of Education in Indiana,* as cited in Thornbrough, *ibid.,* p. 166.

[92] Thornbrough, *op. cit.,* p. 166.

[93] *Ibid.,* p. 323.

[94] *Ibid.,* p. 329.

[95] *Ibid.,* p. 342.

failed to press for their share of the spoils. Although black Republicans were elected to the legislature in 1880, and others occupied seats in the lower house until 1896, not one Negro held a seat between 1896 and 1932, and only a few were even nominated.

Economic Growth and Development

The lasting effects of educational deficiencies and job discrimination served to stunt the economic growth of Negro families, especially when compared to the gains made possible by the technological advancements of the industrial boom following the war. In an effort to overcome their poverty, many blacks migrated to urban areas in search of work. Occupational limitations did little, however, to foster anything but concentrations of unemployed blacks. The vast majority of the Negro population, whether employed or not, was unskilled. Journals of 1890 record only 2,000 skilled Negro workers in the state, the largest proportion of whom were barbers.[96]

Since organized labor excluded Negroes, many blacks resorted to strikebreaking.[97] Efforts at unionization among blacks were sporadic and of short duration, although some all-black independent unions emerged. Most notable was the American Hod Carriers Union in Indianapolis, formed in 1900 by 200 of the city's 350 Negro hod carriers.

With more than 7,300 union members and nine national or international union headquarters, Indianapolis was considered "a stronghold of organized labor."[98] Yet the number of blacks in unions remained insignificant. There were few Negroes in the carpenters' and bricklayers' unions, for instance, and union policies in the city have been cited for being more restrictive than those in larger cities.[99] The discriminatory practices of the

---

[96] W.E.B. DuBois, *The Negro American Artisan*, Atlanta University, Series No. 17, 1912 (Arno Press and *The New York Times* reprint edition), p. 125.

[97] Emma Lou Thornbrough, *Since Emancipation—A Short History of Indiana Negroes, 1863-1963* (Indianapolis: Indiana Division, American Negro Emancipation Centennial Authority, 1963), p. 71.

[98] Clifton J. Phillips, *Indiana in Transition: The Emergence of an Industrial Commonwealth, 1880-1920* (Indianapolis: Indiana Historical Bureau and Indiana Historical Society, 1963), p. 344.

[99] Thornbrough, *Since Emancipation, op. cit.,* p. 79.

unions, in addition to poor educational training, practically precluded blacks from skilled training for fifty years after the Civil War; so effective were the exclusionary policies that while Negroes' educational training improved significantly, occupational opportunities did not do likewise.

1920-1940

The two decades between World Wars I and II brought significant changes to all phases of Indiana's social, economic, and political systems. The influx of blacks from the deep South, initiated in part by the World War I expansion of the steel industry, continued throughout this period, with most Negroes settling in the urban areas. Although Gary was the center of the industrial boom and of the most rapid overall growth, the black population of Indianapolis grew by more than 50 percent in the twenty-year period, and it continued to have the state's largest black population. (Table 26). Migration during World War I and thereafter was so great that by 1930 two-thirds of all Negroes in Indiana had been born outside of the state.[100] The trend of black migration from the farms to the cities (see Table 27), both from within and from outside the state, created new problems and tensions, especially in housing. Middle-income blacks sought to escape the poverty of the ghetto, but expansion meant moving into the "white" areas from which they were usually barred.

Education

Negro school enrollment in Indianapolis rose rapidly during the 1920s and inadequate facilities forced Negroes to attend classes in half-day sessions.[101] The schools were integrated to a small extent, and approximately 1,000 blacks were enrolled in four high schools in 1925.[102] The increase and expansion of the black population brought renewed efforts to the segregation movement in Indianapolis. Parent-teacher associations, the Chamber of Commerce, and neighborhood associations lobbied for a separate high school for Negroes. The City Council yielded

---

[100] Thornbrough, *Since Emancipation, op. cit.*, p. 18.

[101] *Ibid.*, p. 54.

[102] *Ibid.*

TABLE 26. *Indianapolis Plan*
Population of Indianapolis by Race, 1860-1970

Year	Total Population	Negro	Percent Negro
1860	18,611	498	2.7
1870	48,244	2,927	6.1
1880	75,056	6,504	8.7
1890	105,436	9,133	8.7
1900	169,164	15,931	9.4
1910	233,650	21,816	9.3
1920	314,194	34,678	11.0
1930	364,161	43,967	12.1
1940	386,972	51,142	13.2
1950	427,173	63,867	15.0
1960	493,420	98,684	20.0
1970	785,085 [a]	135,000 [a]	17.2

Source: *U.S. Census of Population*

1860: *Eighth Census of the United States*, Indiana, Table III.
1870: *Compendium of the Ninth Census*, Table IX.
1880, 1890, 1900: *Negroes in the United States, 1900*, Table 30.
1910, 1920: Vol. II, *Population*, Table 16.
1930: *Negroes in the United States, 1920-1932*, Table 11.
1940: Vol. II, *Population*, Part II, Table 34.
1950: Vol. II, *Characteristics of the Population*, Part 14, Table 34.
1960: Vol. II, *Characteristics of the Population*, Part 16, Table 20.
1970: *Advance Report on General Population Characteristics*, Indiana.

[a] Indianapolis and Marion County merged in 1970.

TABLE 27. *Indianapolis Plan*
Urban-Rural Distribution of Indiana Negroes
1900-1960

	1900	1930	1960
Percent Negroes in rural area	26.5	8.0	3.4
Percent Negroes in urban area	73.5	92.0	96.6 [a]
	100.0	100.0	100.0

Source: Emma Lou Thornbrough, *Since Emancipation—A Short History of Indiana Negroes, 1863-1963* (Indianapolis: Indiana Division, American Negro Emancipation Centennial Authority, 1963), pp. 18-20; and Clifton J. Phillips, *Indiana in Transition, The Emergence of an Industrial Commonwealth, 1880-1920* (Indianapolis: Indiana Historical Bureau and Indiana Historical Society, 1968), p. 370.

[a] Eighty-five percent of Negroes in 1960 were in seven counties while more than a third of the state's ninety-two counties reported 0-3 Negroes in their population, according to the 1960 census.

to demands and, in 1927, the all-black Crispus Attucks High School opened its doors. The NAACP fought construction of the school, not because of the proposed segregation, but because they felt that "equality" as found in the "separate but equal" doctrine could not be achieved.[103] The State Supreme Court rejected that argument on the basis that premature fears were not grounds for halting construction.[104]

The requirement that all Negroes attend one school caused transportation problems. Many blacks lived in remote areas of the city and could not travel a long distance to school. In 1935 the state legislature required those districts with enforced segregation to provide transportation for Negroes to separate schools.[105]

Politics, Civil Rights, and Economics

The foregoing problems were complicated by the Ku Klux Klan's rise to power in the immediate post-World War I period. Strange

---

[103] *Ibid.*, p. 56.

[104] Emma Lou Thornbrough, "Segregation in Indiana During the Klan Era of the 1920's," *Mississippi Valley Historical Review*, Vol. 47, March 1961, p. 605.

[105] Thornbrough, *Since Emancipation, op. cit.*, p. 37.

as it may appear, no simple cause-and-effect relationship can be established between the Klan's emergence and the increase in legislated restrictions in the black communities. The KKK, as it emerged in Indiana, was antagonistic toward Catholics as well as Negroes.[106] Its attacks were directed primarily at the European immigrants of prewar years who had come with the rise of the industrial centers. This is not to say that Negroes escaped their sting, since Klan doctrine was based on the principal of white supremacy.

Although the Klan drew its following from members of both major political parties, its influence was felt most directly by the Republican party which by 1922 and 1923 had succumbed to its control.[107] The Klan-GOP alliance threatened the long-established alliance of the Negroes and the Republicans, and the 1924 elections found Negroes divided politically.[108] In 1925, Klan-supported candidates won the governorship, control of the state legislature, and the Indianapolis City Council. The fact that no anti-Negro legislation emerged from these agencies, however, brought many Negroes back to the party.[109] Infiltration of government and private agencies by the Klan was so thorough that there is record of it having subsidized one of Indianapolis' black newspapers![110]

Housing and education crises created significant racial tensions in Indianapolis. During this period, the City Council adopted a zoning ordinance aimed at preserving all-white neighborhoods and "stabilizing real estate values" by preventing such property from being sold to Negroes.[111] It was struck down as a result of the United States Supreme Court ruling on a similar Louisiana ordinance.[112] The "white civic league" supporters then resorted to racially restrictive covenants with real estate agents who agreed not to sell white-owned property to Negroes.[113] Such agreements

---

[106] Norman Weaver, "The Knights of the Ku Klux Klan in Wisconsin, Indiana, Ohio, and Michigan," Ph.D. Dissertation, University of Wisconsin, 1954, *passim,* especially pp. 11-31.

[107] Thornbrough, "Segregation in the 1920's," *op. cit.,* p. 609.

[108] *Ibid.,* p. 612.

[109] *Ibid.,* pp. 615-616.

[110] *Ibid.,* p. 612.

[111] *Ibid.,* p. 598.

[112] *Harmon* v. *Tyler,* 273 U.S. 668 (1927).

[113] Thornbrough, *Since Emancipation, op. cit.,* pp. 22-23.

appear to have been effective in containing black residential areas, and, despite some changes, a similar housing pattern still exists.

During the twenties, there were overt clashes between black and white interests. Negro leaders no longer contested the separate-but-equal doctrine, except where equality was threatened, but they did begin to assert their rights in areas not previously tested, such as hotels and theatres.

In the twenties, when the national economy enjoyed a boom period, economic conditions for the Negro improved. In fact, many benefited from a form of reverse discrimination, for "southern Negroes [who as pointed out earlier, were emigrating to this area] were regarded as desirable employees because it was thought that they would be docile and would be less likely to join labor unions than would white workers." [114] However, the Depression erased many of these gains. Traditional policies of "last hired, first fired" significantly affected Negro employment and the number of Negroes on relief rolls steadily increased. The generous relief programs of the New Deal proved to be the severing blow in Negro-Republican alliances, with the elections of 1934 and 1936 revealing massive defections to the Democratic party. As a result, Indianapolis elected its first black Democrat to the City Council, and several Negro Democrats won seats in the state legislature.[115]

Although Negroes made some political gains in the thirties, few economic advances were realized. Building trades unions still excluded blacks from skilled jobs even when governmental authorities promised blacks 12 percent of the skilled jobs on one WPA project.[116] An all-black union of laborers was formed in 1929, but its membership never grew above 300. As a result of union insistence on placing Negroes in unskilled work, cities like Indianapolis reported 60 percent of its Negro men, as opposed to 11 percent of its white men, in unskilled or service-type jobs on the eve of World War II.[117]

1940-1960

Increased production associated with World II brought new jobs and opportunities for Indiana Negroes. Governor Henry

---

[114] *Ibid.*, p. 75.

[115] *Ibid.*, p. 34.

[116] *Ibid.*, p. 76.

[117] *Ibid.*

Schricker set up a biracial committee to help blacks find jobs in defense industries and the President's Committee on Fair Employment Practice (FEPC), established by Presidential executive order, also worked to promote equal employment opportunities. Union attitudes reflected some easing of opposition to black membership, as the Congress of Industrial Organizations (CIO) formally opposed discrimination within its ranks, although its member locals did not always respond accordingly. In 1942, the Carpenters Union issued a charter to an all-black local in Indianapolis, but the building trades unions still effectively barred Negroes in most cases by refusing them admittance to apprenticeship programs.[118] Such all-black locals were generally short-lived.

As the FEPC acted to eliminate discriminatory procedures and practices, pressures arose from militant whites who were fearful of increases in the hiring of blacks. Coupled with a drop in production at the end of the war, this terminated some of the gains made by Negroes in the early forties. Since World War II, Negro membership and influence have risen more markedly in the industrial unions than in the craft unions historically associated with the AFL.[119] "In 1949 it was a newsworthy event when the first Negroes were admitted to a local of the Bricklayers Union." [120] In fact, members of the AFL opposed a proposal before the legislature in 1941 to prohibit discrimination by firms with defense contracts on the grounds that it would weaken collective bargaining.[121]

The anti-segregation drive led by the NAACP was revived during the war, and Indianapolis newspapers and editors gradually backed demands for an end to segregation, charging that the city was the largest northern city with a segregated school system.[122] However, the city school board again adhered to white opponents and delayed such action until 1949, when the state legislature adopted a statewide desegregation bill with biracial, bipartisan, and strong labor support. While some blacks had been attending integrated public schools during the decade because of residential housing patterns and others had been in parochial schools which had been integrated in part as early as 1920, it was not until 1953

---

[118] *Ibid.*, p. 79.

[119] *Ibid.*

[120] *Ibid.*

[121] *Ibid.*, pp. 40-41.

[122] *Indianapolis Star*, February 16, 1947.

that "full" integration was achieved, and even then, it was limited by the neighborhood school concept and racially segregated housing.

Indianapolis, with its substantial black community, escaped much of the racial strife which plagued other large cities during the 1960s. Significant progress had already been made in integrating the educational system and the residential segregation pattern was showing signs of change as minorities attained higher economic levels. Negroes also made substantial gains in local politics, holding elected seats on the city council, and several key appointed posts, including the top two school board posts. Although it was a lengthy process, the Indianapolis minority community by 1970 had established itself in most segments of the city's activities. Skilled jobs for blacks in construction remained a major problem for the 1970s.

CHAPTER VIII

The Evolution of the Indianapolis Plan

An analysis of the Indianapolis hometown plan presents an interesting contrast to the Washington imposed plan. In terms of racial background, the two cities have had quite different experiences. Indianapolis has not witnessed as large a growth in black population as has Washington. Also, while Washington has seen the emergence of a highly centralized black population and many ghetto areas, blacks in Indianapolis have been more or less integrated into the larger community. A strong black coalition in Indianapolis also has had a positive effect on industrial and community race relations.

A "Memorandum of Understanding" creating the Indianapolis Plan was drafted on March 4, 1970 and signed on April 9, 1970. The agreement entered into by representatives of the craft unions, contractors, and the black coalition was in response to the Secretary of Labor's recommendation in February 1970 to establish a national program to achieve equal employment opportunity in federally funded construction work. Nineteen cities, including Indianapolis, were selected and offered a choice of developing hometown plans or following the guidelines of an imposed plan. Indianapolis planners began work in March 1970 with the belief that a locally developed voluntary plan would be an improvement over the imposed Philadelphia-type plan.

THE PLAN AND ITS DEVELOPMENT

Under the guidance of Indianapolis' mayor Richard Lugar and the chairman of the Indianapolis Metropolitan Manpower Commission, Juan C. Solomon, a task force was appointed in February 1970 to develop an agreement in compliance with Executive Order 11246. The task force included the Building Trades Council, the General and Specialty Contractor Association, and the Minority Coalition of Indianapolis. This action group met for five consecutive days and, after considerable deliberation, developed an agreement that would lead to increased participation of minorities on federal and nonfederal construction work. A five-year goal of reaching a level of minority employment in construction at least proportionate to the minority percentage within Indianapolis was agreed upon.

After the general agreement was signed on April 9, 1970, representatives of the unions, contractors, and black community met to negotiate supplemental agreements specifying goals and timetables for minority employment in the particular crafts. By June 4, 1971, all seventeen crafts in Indianapolis had signed agreements.

Building Trades Council

The construction crafts in Indianapolis are loosely joined together in the Marion County Building Trades Council, an organization formed to promote harmony among the crafts and to secure work for union people. The organization was beset with financial crises and internal dissention during the 1950s and substantial craft disaffiliation ensued. However, under the direction of Walter Strough, business agent of the lathers' union, the Council has succeeded in reuniting all seventeen crafts and has eliminated a $10,000 deficit incurred prior to his election in 1959. Although the Council has authority to speak and act for all of its members in certain situations, it cannot, and does not, guarantee member support for its actions. Council spokesmen represented the unions during the discussions and proceedings which developed the framework of the Indianapolis Plan, and it was these spokesmen, acting on behalf of the seventeen crafts, who signed the initial agreement known as the Memorandum of Understanding.

When the negotiations began, the seventeen crafts in the Council represented approximately 8,200 members, of whom less than 300 were minorities. A breakdown by individual craft is presented in Table 28.

Contractor Associations

In Indianapolis there are numerous branches of national contractor associations, whose membership is determined by union or nonunion affiliation, and then by craft. The union contractors include the Building Contractors Association, representing five crafts: carpenters, laborers, ironworkers, cement masons, and operating engineers; the National Electrical Contractors Association; the Sheet Metal Contractors Association; the Mechanical

TABLE 28. *Indianapolis Plan*
Estimated Union Membership of Indianapolis Building Trades
By Race

Craft	Estimated Membership March 1, 1970	Estimated Number of Minorities [a] March 1, 1970	Percent Minority
Asbestos Workers	222	0	—
Bricklayers	422	30	7.1
Carpenters [b]	1,800	37	2.1
Cement Masons	200	140	70.0
Electricians	800	2	0.2
Elevator Constructors	120	2	1.7
Glaziers	87	2	2.3
Ironworkers	788	0 [c]	—
Lathers	100	1	1.0
Operating Engineers	1,200	42	3.5
Painters	366	0	—
Plasterers	95	8	8.4
Plumbers	362	7	1.9
Roofers	275	20	7.3
Sheet Metal Workers	650	1	0.2
Steamfitters	570	0 [c]	—
Tile and Marble Setters	120	5	4.2
Total	8,177	297	3.6

Source: Letter from Indianapolis Plan Project Director, Herman Walker, to Commissioner Juan Solomon, September 17, 1970.

[a] Includes blacks, Chicanos, and Indians.

[b] Includes the membership of five locals involved in the Indianapolis SMSA.

[c] There were two Negroes working on permits, but they were not union members.

Contractors Association; the Lathing and Plastering Contractors Association; the Mason Contractors Association; and the Roofing Contractors Association. In the nonunion sector, the craft qualification is absent since most contractors belong to the Builders Association of Greater Indianapolis, which is affiliated with the National Association of Home Builders.

The union-nonunion division of the contractors also reflects a difference in the type of construction in which each engages. Union contractors handle most of the commercial activity, which includes all elevator buildings and all construction in downtown Indianapolis, while residential work is 95 percent nonunion. Nonunion contractors appear to be gaining a foothold in the commercial sector. They felt little effect of the 1970-1971 economic downturn because of a suburban apartment boom; this caused some bitter resentment on the part of the union contractors, who watched their work drop sharply in this period.

The Black Coalition and Community

The Indianapolis Black Coalition was organized in 1968 when the Model Cities program was started in the city. The Coalition includes the leaders of virtually every black pressure group from the Urban League to the Black Panthers. Its early membership, however, was primarily composed of several church or religious affiliated organizations which sought to put minority workers on the jobs in which Model Cities funds were involved. The influence of the Coalition has grown rapidly and it is now able to offer some semblance of a united front for the entire minority community. Similar coalitions have sprung up in other urban areas across the country where blacks constitute a sizable force in the community, but internal and external politics have subsequently left them split and ineffective.

The Coalition has remained intact from its beginning, despite some internal dissension. Philosophical differences have been made subordinate to the Coalition's basic purposes of keeping leaders in the minority community informed and of using their combined strength to bring about changes in policy affecting the community. David Holt, a member of both the Coalition and the Indianapolis Plan Administrative Committee, as well as business agent for the cement masons' union, cites two reasons for this success: "First, our membership initially evolved from the churches, and I think we got a generally higher calibre of person in the organization, which also manifested itself in the quality of our leadership. Second, we didn't have many chiefs in the beginning like the other cities, just a lot of Indians." [123]

The small size and nonpolitical nature of the Coalition contributed to its early stability. As its sphere of influence gradually embraced the more diversified community organizations, its stability served to discourage bitter leadership rivalries characteristic of other coalitions, which generally tried to organize by bringing together all the diverse elements at once. The Indianapolis Coalition's ability to conduct and control its organization in an orderly manner helped to earn it the respect needed for it to become the voice for its constituencies. Furthermore, so-called radical groups have had little following in the city; this explains in part their willingness to ally with such an organization.

Another factor contributing to the Coalition's success is its refusal to take sides on local political issues on which the minority community is not united. An example of this occurred in 1970 when the city of Indianapolis and surrounding Marion County agreed to merge their governments and services, with the exception of school districts, for more efficient operations. Some black leaders supported the merger on the belief that it was a first step toward progressive local government, while others opposed it on the grounds that it would dilute minority power. The Coalition wisely avoided taking sides, and thereby retained overall support of the black community.

In sum, Indianapolis has a large, active, but moderate black community. Over the past five to ten years, while other urban areas have been torn by racial animosities and riots, this city has managed to avoid any serious disturbances. Geography contributes to the tranquility, for again, unlike other large urban centers, the black community is not confined to just one area, but is scattered throughout the city, although the suburbs remain overwhelmingly white. In such a climate, the Coalition's chances of survival are good, despite its heterogeneous makeup.

The Employment Task Force

The task force of union, contractor, and community representatives called by the mayor to implement a voluntary plan was headed by the Metropolitan Manpower Commissioner, Juan Solomon, a black executive employed by Eli Lilly Pharmaceutical Company. Long active in the local chapter of the NAACP, Solomon was ap-

---

[123] Personal interview, July 21, 1971.

pointed to the Manpower post shortly after Mayor Lugar was elected to his job.

The task force appointed a smaller, tripartite negotiating committee, under the chairmanship of another black, Herman Walker, who was on the staff of the Board for Fundamental Education, a private educational group. This committee met frequently for two weeks and drew up the Indianapolis Plan for Equal Employment (IPEE). The Plan, which finally met the approval of the three groups, was patterned in large measure on the Chicago Plan.

As might be expected, the unions entered the initial hearings of the task force with great reluctance. Most of the business agents were under the impression that their affirmative action plans, drawn up in previous years to meet Department of Labor integration demands, were still sufficient to meet the requirements of the Civil Rights Act and Executive Order 11246. However, they were prevailed upon by both contractors and some union leaders to participate in the proceedings to develop a voluntary plan, which was thought to be the lesser of the two evils that the "either-or" directive left open to them.

Early discussions of the Plan were further complicated by the attendance of a fourth group at the initial proceedings— the nonunion contractors of the Builders Association of Greater Indianapolis (BAGI). It soon became evident that their presence in the planning sessions had served to create a three-way argument between the unions and the union and nonunion contractors. The union-nonunion conflict at the planning table thus caused an intolerable situation from the standpoint of developing a plan, since any potential agreement between the Coalition and the unions would require rather delicate maneuvering, and this was impossible with BAGI representatives in attendance. Hence, they were asked to withdraw from the proceedings.[124]

The Memorandum of Understanding, the document drawn up and agreed to by the three parties on the negotiations committee, outlines the purposes and administrative structure of the proposed operations. Unlike the design of the original Philadelphia Plan, this agreement covers all construction activity of member contractors, not just federal or federally assisted con-

---

[124] A separate plan later developed by BAGI to cover its contractors remains unsigned by the Indianapolis Plan staff, because it fears that such a plan would be in competition with that for the unions and would hence threaten any future "achievements" of minority employment in the commercial or union sector.

struction. When the nonunion sector was eliminated from participation, the Indianapolis Plan appeared to afford the unions a significant advantage in future awardings of contracts with federal money which no doubt was an incentive for them to participate.

THE PLAN AND ITS ADMINISTRATION

The Memorandum, agreed to in March and formally approved on April 9, 1970, states the overall goal of the Plan to be the achievement over a five-year period of a level of minority employment in the construction crafts equal to the minority groups' percentage of the population in Marion County.[125] The document also sets forth the administrative organization of the Plan; this includes an administrative committee to coordinate and direct the program, and sixteen [126] subordinate operations committees through which the coordination and direction are to be exercised.

The Memorandum of Understanding further specifies four categories of construction workers—Journeyman, Advanced Trainee, Apprentice, and Trainee—which are defined as follows:

1. *Journeymen*—those qualified persons possessing the necessary skills of their respective trade.
2. *Advance Trainees*—those persons possessing some of the skills of a particular trade, capable of furnishing proof of employment for two or more years in a particular craft. They shall receive special job-related education.
3. *Apprentices*—Individuals with no prior training, not possessing the skills of a particular craft, but within the age limits for entering into specified intensive training programs for a particular craft. Such persons would be prepared for entering the existing apprenticeship programs of all crafts, and would be subject to meeting all craft union specifications.
4. *Trainees*—Persons who do not wish to take the apprenticeship tests for admission into the respective crafts, or who fail in such tests, or who do not meet the basic eligibility requirements of each program. The recruits will receive on-the-job training and job-related education.

---

[125] "Memorandum of Understanding," April 9, 1970.

[126] The Plan covers seventeen crafts, but two, the lathers and plasterers, **meet** jointly as one.

Traditional union classifications, with few exceptions, are limited to apprentices and journeymen, and despite the presence of labor representatives at the drafting sessions, the new proposed four-level system evoked neither discussion nor dissent. In fact, the only open union opposition was voiced by the carpenters, who argued that the long-range goal of proportionate representation for minorities constituted a quota, and thus was in violation of Title VII of the 1964 Civil Rights Act. The Building Trades Council, however, dismissed the carpenters' dissent and signed the agreement as drafted.

Administrative Committee

The Administrative Committee functions like any corporation's board of directors; it is charged with implementing and monitoring the Plan, and its duties include dealing with the problems of finances, administration, and recalcitrant participants. The Committee meets at least once a month and is headed by the mayor or his representative and has twelve other voting members, four each from the Building Trades Council, the contractor organizations, and the minority coalition. Because of his initial work with the Plan, Juan Solomon was selected by Mayor Lugar to fill the chairman's seat.

Operations Committees

The operations committees are designed to be the more specialized functionaries of the Plan. They are charged with the routine problems such as training, recruiting, referral, and publicity for each of the crafts. Although scheduled to meet once a month, the committees have frequently found it necessary to convene more often to handle the many complex responsibilities. More significantly, these committees were initially given the task of developing the individual supplemental agreements which outlined each craft's numerical goals for minority placements, a function which occasionally proved to be a lengthy ordeal, especially in the case of the carpenters.

These committees are also tripartite in organization, with two representatives each from the unions and contractors, and four from the Coalition. A degree of uniformity in the actual operations of the committees was achieved by placing the same four coalition members on each of the sixteen operations committees.

Indianapolis Plan Staff

Shortly after the formal signing of the Memorandum, the Administrative Committee began the task of finding a director for the Plan. Under the provisions of the Department of Labor contract which funds the program, a director and seven-man staff are authorized to provide the day-to-day supervision and coordination of the activities of the operations committees, while also aiding them in the recruitment, testing, and selection of applicants. The staff includes four counselor-recruiters, an education specialist, and three clerks. Herman Walker, a participant in most of the negotiations of the Memorandum and the early operations committees meetings, was appointed director.

The four recruiter positions were filled by the following individuals: the Reverend Don Bundles and the Reverend Tom Petty, both "borrowed" from local automobile plants; Frank Smith, a former highway inspector; and Launcelot Jones, Associate Director of the Indianapolis-Marion County Commission on Human Rights. The post of Education Director was filled by Joe O'Neill from the sheet-metal workers' union. O'Neill served only three or four months and was replaced by James Cooper, president of the lathers' local union. This staffing process was completed in May and June of 1970 and it was not until July 1 that the funding of the staff's operation actually commenced.

DEVELOPMENT OF SUPPLEMENTAL AGREEMENTS

As noted earlier, the Memorandum of Understanding was drawn up in March and signed by all parties on April 9, 1970. Some five weeks of intensive discussion and negotiation were necessary to obtain the commitment of each group. The document dealt with none of the highly controversial topics such as numbers of minorities, training program specifics, or personnel classifications; but it did establish a sound administrative base from which to begin operations. The Memorandum of Understanding alone did not constitute an acceptable voluntary plan; without the formal commitment of the participants in supplemental agreements, it was only an expression of general intent and in need of more specific objectives and plans.

Controversial topics were left to the operations committees to resolve and following the April ratification of the general agreement, these committees tackled the problems. The first few meetings of each were devoted more to getting acquainted than to business. Union and contractor representatives usually knew one another beforehand, but the minorities on the committees were strangers and these sessions were primarily aimed at developing a spirit of cooperation and trust.

Once it was felt that the channels were open, each committee selected a chairman and the negotiations over goals and policies began. The initial supplemental agreements covered two construction sessions and a time period of a year and a half. For funding purposes, this accounted for two of the five years during which the Indianapolis Plan was to function.

Coalition representatives based their demands on the unions for minority placements on the estimated minority percentage of the population, since the 1970 census figures had not then been released. An understanding was reached that once census figures became available, adjustments would be made in the crafts' goals.

In less than a month, seven crafts signed agreements, and by the end of June another five had come to terms. In late June, the Department of Labor reviewed the initial supplemental agreements, found them acceptable as to goals and method of implementation, and approved the Indianapolis Plan for funding purposes. Approval was somewhat contingent on the participation of the yet unsigned crafts, four of which were considered critical trades in which there were few minorities nationwide. With the approval of funds, the IPEE staff was formally established and began to operate by assuming some of the functions which the Coalition had heretofore conducted, in addition to those duties prescribed for them.

Negotiations with the five unsigned crafts continued during the summer, and by mid-September only the carpenters remained nonsignatory. After considerable pressure, the carpenters signed in early June of 1971. The total goal for the 1970-1971 construction seasons, as established by the operations committees, was jobs for approximately 500 minorities (Table 29).

TABLE 29. *Indianapolis Plan*
Minority Goals by Craft

Craft	Date Signed	1970-71 Goal
Lathers	May 5, 1970	10
Plasterers	May 5, 1970	10
Roofers	May 8, 1970	20
Tile and Marble Setters	May 18, 1970	16
Sheet Metal Workers	May 18, 1970	20
Plumbers	May 20, 1970	30
Operating Engineers	May 21, 1970	50
Painters	June 5, 1970	40
Steamfitters	June 9, 1970	40
Glaziers	June 10, 1970	10
Asbestos Workers	June 15, 1970	30
Cement Masons	June 30, 1970	20
Electricians	August 24, 1970	60
Brickmasons	August 25, 1970	40
Elevator Constructors	September 8, 1970	12
Ironworkers	September 11, 1970	40
Carpenters	June 4, 1971	140 [a]
Total		518 [b]

Source: Indianapolis Plan for Equal Employment.

[a] 1971-1972 goal.

[b] Excludes 70 of carpenters' 1972 goal.

AN OVERVIEW: FALL 1970-SPRING 1972

Following completion of the negotiations with all crafts except the carpenters, the IPEE staff was able to devote full attention to the task of placing minorities. The 1970 construction season was good, but not equal to the record-breaking level of the year before. Between July and December, almost 150 minorities were placed in jobs, but few continued to work through the slack winter season.

The staff spent the winter season trying to anticipate the needs of the local crafts for the next year and then recruiting potential workers to have available once work began. An extensive program to train minorities as operating engineers was conducted in March at a cost to the Plan of almost $50,000. Referred to as the Sky Harbor Project, it was hoped to be a model for future training programs in other crafts, but the costs made that prohibitive. Consequently, less capital-oriented programs were developed during the summer.

Negotiations with the carpenters continued sporadically for several months, and Walker finally requested assistance from the Department of Labor in January 1971. Before the Labor Department answered Walker's request, equal employment inspectors from federal agencies visited several large construction sites in Indianapolis and decided to hold up the beginning of the Indiana University-Purdue University Extension complex, the largest building project planned for the city. This action broke the carpenters' resistance and they signed an agreement with the Plan; however, the problems with the craft did not end quickly, as disagreements arose over how to implement this aspect of the Plan.

As the summer of 1971 progressed, it became evident that the economic slump was much sharper than predicted; in mid-July, every craft still had men on the bench, and in August, the brickmasons claimed that only 50 percent of their 400 men were working. Minority placements fell far behind projections and by December only another 100 had been added to the work force.

In September, Herman Walker left the Plan to take a position with the Housing and Urban Development Department (HUD). The Administrative Committee appointed Albert Butler, Director of Economic Development and Merit Employment for the Urban League and one of the four minority representatives on the operations committees, as Walker's successor. Butler had served on the Administrative Committee since its formation, thus bringing with him an intimate knowledge of the Plan's development. Bid requirements for nonparticipants of the Indianapolis Plan were also published by the Department of Labor in September. The impact of these bid conditions is discussed later in this volume.

The Indianapolis Plan has since undergone its first formal review by government officials. In January and March of 1972, equal employment representatives of major federal agencies visited the city, the staff offices, various construction sites, and the operations committees of each craft. As a result of their findings, investigators placed all but two crafts on probation until June when another such review was planned.

CHAPTER IX

The Indianapolis Plan: An Evaluation

When this study was initiated, the Indianapolis Plan was little more than a year old. Although one craft had not signed a supplemental agreement, the Plan was functioning for the remaining sixteen. During the last six months of 1970, the Indianapolis Plan for Equal Employment claimed credit for placing 135 minorities in jobs,[127] and there were high expectations of reaching established goals.

ANALYSIS OF PLACEMENTS

A total of 290 placements were made by the Plan in 1970-1971, including 42 journeymen, 46 advanced trainees, 135 trainees, and 67 apprentices. As pointed out earlier, projections of work for 1970-1971 failed to materialize, and by December 31, 1971, despite participation of all crafts, the Plan was 228 placements short of its goal (Table 30). Only two of the seventeen crafts, the ironworkers and roofers, managed to exceed their goals.

The poor construction seasons in 1970 and 1971 did little to encourage minority hiring by the crafts, and opposition of some trades, which already had men on the bench, was stiffened. The carpenters, electricians, sheet metal workers, operating engineers, and bricklayers complained bitterly about adding to those already unemployed, and they have resisted doing so whenever possible or necessary. By the end of 1971, the first four of the above mentioned five crafts accounted for almost 60 percent of the 228 placements not made.

Lack of success in placing minorities in some cases was not solely the result of bad faith efforts or poor seasons. The cement masons' union was already 70 percent black when the Plan began. The lathers and glaziers were crafts on the decline, and the bricklayers had a significant number of journeymen on the bench. Although placements in these crafts are necessary for compliance

---

[127] Monthly Progress Report of the Indianapolis Plan for Equal Employment, December 31, 1970.

TABLE 30. *Indianapolis Plan*
Minority Placements by Craft
1970-1971

Craft	Journeymen	Advanced Trainees	Trainees	Apprentices	Total Number of Placements	Goal	Number over (or short of Goal)
Asbestos Workers	0	0	3	10	13	30	(17)
Bricklayers	4	0	0	0	4	40	(36)
Carpenters	13	0	3	9	25	70[a]	(45)
Cement Masons	1	0	0	3	4	20	(16)
Electricians	0	3	27	7	37	60	(23)
Elevator Constructors	0	0	8	0	8	12	(4)
Glaziers	0	0	6	0	6	10	(4)
Ironworkers	1	38	0	8	47	40	7
Lathers	0	1	0	3	4	10	(6)
Operating Engineers	10	0	3	9	22	50	(28)
Painters	2	1	17	12	32	40	(8)
Plasterers	2	2	1	0	5	10	(5)
Plumbers	4	1	8	0	13	30	(17)
Roofers	5	0	18	0	23	20	3
Sheet Metal Workers	0	0	0	6	6	20	(14)
Steamfitters	0	0	30	0	30	40	(10)
Tile Setters	0	0	11	0	11	16	(5)
Total	42	46	135	67	290	518	228
Other (Non-Construction)							
Truck Drivers	0	0	5	0	5		
Electronics	0	0	2	0	2		
Carpet Layers	1	0	0	0	1		

Source: December 31, 1971, "Placement Summary Report for the Indianapolis Plan."

[a] Goal for 1971 only.

reasons, these trades have not been pressured as much as the skilled, growing trades, where the long-range employment outlook is good, but where current minority membership is negligible.

A Look into 1972

The 1972 construction season began early in Indianapolis, indicating a strong comeback from the past two recession-like years for the local industry. Table 31 reveals the placement progress made by the Plan through September 1972. Considerable placement activity has occurred in 1972, reflecting an improved economic position in the industry and renewed efforts by the Plan's participants as a result of audits by the federal government. In the first nine months of 1972, the following additions were made in the Plan: 22 journeymen, 6 advanced trainees, 190 trainees, and 52 apprentices. Further follow-up will be necessary to determine the true effectiveness of the placements in terms of continued employment. The fact that four trades—asbestos workers, bricklayers, glaziers, and painters—have recently been placed under the bid conditions may generate further action by those who have been reluctant to participate fully with the Plan.

QUALITATIVE ANALYSIS

It is difficult to analyze the success of any program in the early stages of its development and implementation. The foregoing has attempted to show how well the Indianapolis Plan has operated toward bringing minorities into the construction crafts. In addition to the analysis of statistical data, it is necessary to consider other aspects of the Plan which determine the environment in which placements are made. Such matters as staffing, administration, and internal procedures, the nature of training programs, duration of employment, and union, contractor, and community attitudes toward the Plan are discussed below.

The Administrative Committee

As the titular head of the Indianapolis Plan, the Administrative Committee meets monthly to review the operations of the staff and individual crafts. Representatives from the Bureau of Apprenticeship and Training, the AFL-CIO Human Resources Development Institute, and the ironworkers' training program, attend monthly meetings as an advisory group. Although the committee is vested with broad powers, it has been reluctant to

TABLE 31. *Indianapolis Plan*
Minority Placements by Craft
through September 1972

Craft	Journeymen	Advanced Trainees	Trainees	Apprentices	Total Number of Placements
Asbestos Workers	0	0	16	11	27
Bricklayers	4	0	0	5	9
Carpenters	40	1	34	14	89
Cement Masons	1	0	0	11	12
Electricians	0	3	67	7	77
Elevator Constructors	0	0	12	5	17
Glaziers	0	0	6	0	6
Ironworkers	1	42	0	10	53
Lathers	0	1	3	6	10
Operating Engineers	3	0	22	21	46
Painters	2	2	27	16	47
Plasterers	3	2	5	2	12
Plumbers	4	1	28	0	33
Roofers	6	0	28	0	34
Sheet Metal Workers	0	0	13	9	22
Sprinklerfitters	0	0	1	2	3
Steamfitters	0	0	52	0	52
Tile Setters	0	0	11	0	11
Total	64	52	325	119	560

Source: September 1972, "Placement Summary Report for the Indianapolis Plan."

exercise authority in a manner that might appear to be controversial. It has approved all supplemental agreements negotiated by the Plan's staff and has generally turned over control to the staff. Meetings over the past year appear to have been perfunctory and held mainly to comply with rules that specify periodic meetings. Absenteeism has been high, and several vacancies have occurred since the initial representatives were appointed. One union vacancy remained open for more than a year.[128]

The March 1971 review of the Plan conducted by the Office of Federal Contract Compliance (OFCC) appears to have enlivened the Committee. In fact, Coalition representatives tried in March to persuade the Committee to recommend that several crafts be held in noncompliance and thus placed under government-determined bid requirements. They came within one vote of succeeding.[129] The proposal, oddly enough, was made over the objections of fellow Coalition members on the Plan's staff who felt that such action was unwarranted at this point. The staff favored, instead, a recommendation from the OFCC reviewer which gave most crafts three months to produce results or else face such action as the Coalition members had recommended. Whether the split in opinion among the Coalition on this subject will carry over into other matters remains to be seen, but it is the first visible evidence of dissent to be expressed at the Administrative Committee meetings.

Because the Committee has not yet had to act on any major issues it has avoided any formal polarization of ideas and a somewhat informal and relaxed atmosphere in which to discuss problems has been preserved. If the government initially determines which crafts are not in compliance and then formally requests the committee to take over the function, it will be more capable of handling such an inflammable subject than it would if it acted on its own. Since most crafts and contractors view it as a remote element in the Plan, the Committee commands neither respect nor fear. An attempt to exercise authority which few actually know it has might be more harmful than beneficial.

---

[128] The vacancy resulted from the death of Carl Wall of the bricklayers' union in spring, 1971.

[129] Minutes of the Administrative Committee Meeting, Friday, March 17, 1971.

The Coalition/Indianapolis Plan Staff

Early negotiations of the Plan were dominated by Coalition members, who because they sat on all operations committees, were the constants in an otherwise variable area. The Administrative Committee exercised little supervision over the early negotiations, thus allowing the Coalition a certain amount of freedom at the bargaining table. Since three of the four Coalition bargainers eventually took jobs on the Indianapolis Plan staff, they brought to that body a degree of expertise and intimate familiarity with the proceedings leading to the general and supplemental agreements. This was extremely important in that the staff of the Plan was not formally created until June 30, 1970, nearly three months after approval of the Memorandum of Understanding and after agreements with twelve crafts had been negotiated and accepted.

In their dual role of being Coalition representatives and day-to-day administrators of the Plan, the staff has had to be very flexible, creative, and mobile. When negotiations of the supplemental agreements began, the Coalition members were familiar with the proceedings leading up to that point, and they had to provide other committee members with the necessary background information. They have also had to steer operations committees along the most productive path. Without the Coalition, negotiations of supplemental agreements could have been forever entangled over terminology, intent, expectations, and irrelevant details.

The Coalition bargainers were guided by Herman Walker, who has been intimately involved in the labor movement and whose personal dynamics dominated the early development of the Plan. His ability to speak the unions' language and his commitment to the success of voluntarism made him a logical choice to direct the staff. Walker made it known from the outset that he wanted no special favors for minorities; rather, he wanted them to have the same opportunities as everyone else. If, for example, there were two entry routes into the union, he wanted both completely open. As long as such routes were not institutionally biased against minorities, he never attacked the union's system, choosing instead to work within it.

In the first few months of the Plan's operation, Walker established himself as the main force behind it. Every union leader and almost every contractor knew of him, and few were willing or even had reason to challenge him. As long as negotiations were conducted in an open and reasonable manner, there was little need for confrontation. In fact, overcoming pessimism within the Coalition was often more difficult.[130]

Negotiations of supplemental agreements were among the least complex tasks to which the Coalition and staff have been assigned. They were also required to set up the administrative machinery of the voluntary Plan, including development of internal procedures, formal recruiting channels, and methods of maintaining contact with anyone placed under the Plan. These duties had to be performed at a time when negotiations with five important skilled crafts were still in process. During the early months of the Plan's development, the staff was further burdened by the necessity to devote substantial time and effort to the physical placement of minorities. Little guidance was offered by the sponsoring federal agency during this period.

The staff also had to determine such things as which records and what information ought to be kept or obtained for personal files and for government reporting purposes. Walker, for example, had to seek advice from personal friends in government agencies as far away as Chicago in order to determine how to complete some of the required monthly activity reports. Information and assistance on proper reporting and budgetary procedures had never been provided to the staff and valuable time was lost in trying to work out problems associated with these matters.

The monthly reports submitted by the staff during the first year contained errors which should have been corrected by a monitoring agency.[131] Neither the local office of the Bureau of Apprenticeship and Training, which monitored the reports for the first six months, nor the federal agencies directly in charge of the Plan audited reports closely enough to eliminate mistakes.

Fortunately, the staff members were able initially to develop a basic set of internal documents which were comprehensive and in need of only slight modification as time progressed. A personal folder is maintained at the IPEE office for each applicant placed. Information concerning the individual, his skill training, and work performance are recorded. The initial application for work also is retained as well as any record of a

---

[130] Personal interview, Herman Walker, June 29, 1971.

[131] An examination of monthly activity reports submitted to Washington reveals basic errors in the reporting of total placements and placements by individual crafts.

personal visit by the staff with the individual whether for routine or for counseling purposes. The work performance record contains a weekly reporting of an individual's hours worked and the contractor for whom he worked, along with any comments from either the employer or employee concerning the work. Training records are maintained that contain academic evaluations of minorities enrolled in apprentice or job-related education programs conducted by the local crafts, skill centers, and/or the IPEE staff.

The collection of information on an individual basis is important for those participants in the Plan who eventually expect to be elevated to the position of journeyman in the union. Record keeping provides minorities with the necessary proof of employment and contractor references that will be needed to make application to journeyman status. If an individual is rejected, the records will provide the government with tools to effect integration of the crafts through appropriate measures. Thus, by centralizing and standardizing the information necessary for such future activity, the staff is laying the foundation for future entrance of minorities into the trades in a manner which has traditionally been reserved for whites.

Staff Operations

Unlike the imposed Washington Plan, the Indianapolis Plan is a more visible, tangible entity. It has a full-time director, employees working on a permanent basis, and a conveniently located downtown office. All potential applicants for the Plan recruited either by the operations committees or by the staff working through various neighborhood and community agencies (NAACP, Model Cities, Urban League) are directed to the office to complete a formal written application and to determine areas of interest. The Plan has been an accessible, people-oriented institution from the beginning.

Once the placement activities of the staff began in the summer of 1970, staff members made weekly visits to job sites to talk with minorities and the contractors who employed them. If an individual was found to be late for work or having difficulty in getting along on the job, staff members attempted to discover the reasons for such behavior and provide counseling to help overcome problems. Walker explained to both the applicants and the contractors hiring them that he was not interested in placing faces on job sites for the sake of meeting a quota, nor did he want any minorities on jobs who felt that they would not be fired because of their race.

Walker encouraged contractors to keep the staff informed of problems so that they could be corrected at an early stage. After a few such requests and quick responses, employers were convinced that Walker was serious about conducting a quality program. Some contractors initially labored under the conviction that "once hired, a minority cannot be fired," sensing that Walker's words were stronger than his actions. This idea was cast aside by an incident involving an electrical contractor who found a participant in the Plan stealing on the job. Not knowing what to do, but fearing some retaliation if he reacted harshly, the contractor sent the man home but did not fire him. He called the IPEE to inform them of the situation and a staff member visited the accused individual to hear his story. Subsequent to the meeting, Walker requested the contractor to fire the man.[132] This action gave the contractors confidence in the Plan's hiring process and made them more willing to hire additional men, for they knew that they still retained the right to hire or fire, regardless of race.

Weekly visits to construction sites also provide the staff with firsthand knowledge of the local industry problems. As staff member Don Bundles explained, "It made us more aware of the individual problems with which the employers and unions were dealing and gave us a more common footing for the discussions at the operations committee meetings, for then we were all working from a base of familiarity with the problems." [133] These visits have reduced the potential for extremist demands on either side and have inspired an attitude of reasonableness and reality during the meetings.

In addition to visiting contractors who have hired minorities through the Plan, staff members also make regular checks with contractors who have not hired minorities. Their approach has been rational, although it has drawn some criticism from the black community representatives who feel that not enough is happening. Staff members have not asked contractors to lay off whites in order to hire minorities, choosing instead to ask contractors to fill vacancies with minorities; at the same time, contract award proceedings are monitored to obtain information as to which contractors will be hiring and thus have potential opportunities for minorities.

---

[132] As related by Bob Baldus, NECA president, July 13, 1972.

[133] Personal interview, July 27, 1971.

The procedures developed by the Plan can produce significant results in prosperous periods. In 1970 and 1971, however, unemployment in the crafts was as high as 40 percent in peak season and up to 80 percent in the winter, despite technological improvements which allow year-round work in most crafts. Because of poor economic conditions in the industry, numerical results have not been overwhelming; but there has been a moral victory, in that contractors display little hesitance in conferring with the staff on future work and possible hires.

One might argue that numerical results would have been better under an imposed plan, but under such circumstances there would be no permanent communications channel between the Coalition-community and the employers. If voluntarism is to succeed, it must bridge the gap between peaks in construction activity so as to maintain viability during the depressions and prepare for the next peak. Success also will be founded somewhat on the sense of obligation the parties feel toward one another. The strong rapport already established between the parties enhances the opportunity for placements if the comeback for the commercial construction industry predicted for 1972 materializes.[134]

The increasing number of minorities being hired has made weekly contact with each individual almost impossible. Routine checks with contractors employing minorities are now made with the use of a standard form drafted by the Plan for such purposes. The form provides the staff with information such as who is currently working, the reasons why individuals have been laid off, and an evaluation of each person's performance. The staff continues its policy of personal contact with newly placed workers until they feel each can perform without further help or advice.

The Operations Committees

Although designed to be key activists of a voluntary plan, most operations committees have been somewhat more passive than intended, but this is not their fault alone. The slump in commercial work and the resulting industry-wide unemployment created a difficult environment for talk of increased opportunities for minorities; moreover, the staff of the Indianapolis Plan has taken on some of the duties initially envisioned as being the responsibility of these committees.

---

[134] Interview with Richard Nye, Associate Director of Area Development, Indianapolis Chamber of Commerce, January 21, 1972.

Each committee selected its own leader and in all but one case a contractor was chosen.[135] Being in the more neutral position between the union and the Coalition, the contractors were the logical choice for the post, and seldom was more than one person nominated. Although the chairman should be the person who sets the prevailing mood for the committee's operations, the position is not one which carries with it particular power, an extra vote, or additional encumbering responsibilities. Hence it is not one which any party should actively seek or show discontent if he fails to win, nor is it a post which anyone should desire to avoid. The Coalition has thus had the opportunity to display its reasonableness to the unions and contractors by supporting one of them for the post.

After the committees were organized, the first order of business was the development of goals. For some crafts, it proved an extended process covering three to five months (the carpenters' negotiations actually took one year); for others it was a matter of only a few meetings before an agreement was reached. The problems faced in the negotiations focused basically on two areas: (1) getting the unions to agree to a definite number of placements, and (2) incorporating the trainee and advanced trainee concept into existing union structures.

Since the Coalition members had participated in the development of the Memorandum of Understanding, they were in a position to explain the terminology and intent of the document to committee members. Since the same Coalition members sat on every committee, there was a certain degree of uniformity in the dialogue. Emphasis was placed on the concept of voluntarism and how it relates to satisfaction of equal opportunity compliance requirements. Each committee was told that development of a voluntary plan that met with OFCC's approval would mean no interference from compliance officers. Contractors and union representatives generally looked with favor upon any proposal which will alleviate such pressures and eliminate threats of job-site shutdowns. Additional incentive for them to participate in the Plan lay in the implication that if they could meet equal employment requirements, they stood to gain federal contracts which nonsignatory, nonunion contractors had previously received. It was assumed that the latter would be extremely hard-pressed to get into compliance.

---

[135] The electricians' operations committee chose the union business agent as its head.

Unions were informed also that numerical goals were not the only criteria upon which performance would be evaluated; in a sense, the impact of specific goals was lessened. They were told instead that evaluation and judgment would be rendered on the basis of their efforts to reach the goal. Voluntarism was to be much more flexible than the seemingly rigid requirements of an imposed solution.

The approach of the Coalition representatives in the negotiations was predicated upon two hypotheses: (1) that contractors would be more receptive than unions to any negotiations because of the direct or personal economic threat of noncompliance; and (2) that union bargainers had to be offered some evidence that they would fare better under a voluntary plan than under an imposed solution.[136] The latter was a particularly difficult concept to put across with union representatives, who are elected officials of the locals and therefore accountable to the members and subject to "ballot-box eviction." Many were reluctant to sign their name voluntarily to any document. This accentuated the need for an effective presentation of the advantages of voluntarism.

Negotiations of the supplemental agreements differed from craft to craft because of situations peculiar to each craft, but a general pattern evolved since the Coalition members sat on every committee. The meaning of voluntarism and of the goals outlined in the Memorandum of Understanding were first thrashed about until it was felt that all participants understood the situation.

In the beginning, some problems did occur over the classification of workers. The operating engineers', for example, had a job progression system through which its members normally moved, beginning with the low skilled oilers and advancing to the highly skilled operators. The union initially viewed the Plan as proposing to set up four categories at each step in the job progression, a situation which would produce chaos, especially in the training programs. The union already had problems with some members wanting to remain permanently as oilers, for the pay was good, and the work was relatively easy; but this had the effect of forcing the local to place apprentices at higher skill levels from the outset. The idea of segregating each job level with four categories, as the union

---

[136] Interview with Herman Walker, July 13, 1971.

thought the Plan would, consequently angered their representatives.

The carpenters claimed that their International constitution
permitted only two classes of workers, journeymen and apprentices. They argued that they could not accept a proposal
which specified two additional classifications, trainees and advanced trainees, since neither the rules nor their training program would allow it. The asbestos workers' business agent
argued in the same manner, but his craft did not even have a
recognized apprenticeship program approved by the Bureau
of Apprenticeship and Training. Ironworkers' representatives
claimed that none of the proposals would apply to them because
their International had its own program to aid minorities, which
was approved by the U.S. Department of Labor.

Coalition members seized upon the asbestos workers' situation as a chance to demonstrate their abilities to work with the
crafts by offering help in developing an apprenticeship program
which would meet the Bureau of Apprenticeship and Training
standards. The craft's contractors had been asking for the
program for several years but had received little response from
the union which operated an informal and unapproved training
program. A similar solution was applied to the Cement Masons,
although their participation in the Plan was practically guaranteed since their union was 70 percent black and their business
agent was on the Administrative Committee. The Operating
Engineers' doubts were settled with an explanation of the Plan's
proposed operations; in addition, the Coalition affirmed their
support of the union's efforts to prevent clustering in the low-
skilled jobs. The four levels of training remained a stumbling
point for over a year in the carpenters' union; the categories
of trainees and advanced trainees were eventually retitled "special apprentices" and "second-year apprentices."

Once the classification of prospective placements was resolved,
the numerical goals had to be established. Union representatives
naturally wanted to deflate the goals; the Coalition wanted them
as high as possible, and the contractors vacillated, opting for
almost any solution which might prevent loss of federal contracts.
This application of tripartitism is worthy of further analysis
in that its practice differs from the historical precedent.

Tripartitism of a New Kind [137]

In contrast to the traditional workings of tripartitism, the public or community representatives (the Coalition) sitting on the operations committees of the Plan are not neutral members. They occupy the place at the bargaining table which labor has traditionally held, making demands on the union to employ their people. If the Coalition had been weak, its demands would have gone unheeded, without direct government intervention, just as a weak union's demands would be ignored by management where possible.

In their role as neutrals, the contractors are subject to additional pressures which are usually not evident in tripartite situations in industrial relations. The new pressures are the result of contractors having personal stakes in the determination of a solution, because they must abide by federal requirements in order to win contracts. At the same time, they must continue to cooperate with the union, for it controls the worker input.

A detailed look at each of the three parties reveals how this tripartite system developed:

Contractors.　Contractors have had the most substantial burden of any of the three participants in the Plan. More jobs were to be provided for minorities and the contractors had a chance to determine how many. This was important to them, since they would feel the immediate economic impact of hiring and paying individuals, many of whom might lack formal craft training and would require the day-to-day help of skilled craftsmen already on the job.

The reaction of contractor members of the committees to the initial negotiations of supplemental agreements ranged from support of the Plan to support of union resistance, but the general trend was for the contractors to attempt to mediate any union-Coalition conflict. In most cases, disagreement arose over the question of the actual number of jobs to which the craft would commit itself, and the contractors were usually able to effect a compromise.

Contractors did not assume the role of mediators in every case. Electrical contractors, who were afraid of union retaliation, refused to intercede until the Coalition threatened them with

---

[137] The most notable examples of the practice of tripartitism in this country occurred during World Wars I and II with the National War Labor Boards and during the Korean War with the Wage Stabilization Board. The Nixon Administration's original Pay Board is a similar type of organization.

an imposed plan.[138] Even then, although a small wedge had been driven between the union and the contractors, it was not until the electrical contractor association leadership changed that any mediatory efforts were made. Contractor representatives on the carpenters' committee have been equally as weak in their participation. Since contractors were willing to sign any document specifying a number, the union was angered and, in turn, discounted any employer input once this became evident. Negotiations in this craft became a test of power between the union and the Coalition, a struggle which ended only after the federal government made its presence known by curtailing activity at a large construction site for noncompliance with equal employment regulations. The attitude of the contractors on the electricians' and carpenters' operations committees was the exception rather than the rule, however, for most employers tried to participate effectively from the beginning.

Unions. Union reaction to the Plan also was varied. Resistance was strong in the all-white, highly skilled trades and weak in trades with minorities already in the membership or with a tradition of minority opportunity. Initial opposition from the electricians was philosophical; opposition from the painters appeared to be entirely personal,[139] and from the carpenters came both types of resistance, in addition to the initial challenge that goals as stated in the Plan were legally invalid.[140]

Support from other crafts was based on diverse reasons. Walter Strough, representative of the Lathers and President of the Building Trades Council, wanted to set an example for other crafts and to demonstrate organized labor's support of nondiscriminatory opportunities.[141] The glaziers were shown how additional pressures would be created on unorganized shop men to join their craft if union-oriented minorities were placed there. The brickmasons' support came after they received assurances from the IPEE staff that it would initially help to find work for minorities already in the trade but on the bench.

Union business agents, who sat on the committees, objected most strenuously to the Plan's goals. Few wanted to place them-

---

[138] As noted earlier, this was the only committee which elected a union official as its chairman.

[139] William Lumreid, business agent for the painters' union, resigned his post rather than participate in negotiations of a supplemental agreement.

[140] A more detailed look at the Carpenters appears later in the chapter.

[141] Personal interview with Walter Strough, July 27, 1971.

selves in a position of having to defend their signed approval of the Plan without first obtaining some reduction in the Coalition's goals. They were not strong enough politically within the locals to act without sounding out the membership for guidance and/or planning their defense first.

As long as there is an increasing work volume, unions are not likely to oppose restrictions on membership; but where the industry workload is sagging, politics can reassert itself as a significant factor. If local union leaders are to make decisions contrary to the wishes of the membership, they must have someone to blame. The government, which holds the threat of an imposed plan over the heads of those who resist voluntary efforts, has become their "whipping boy."

Coalition. The Coalition has had to exercise great caution at the bargaining table. While demanding placements for minorities, it must avoid threatening union leaders with an imposed plan. Under continued threats, the unions might believe that the imposed plan is a more viable and face-saving alternative no matter how much they dislike the federal government. The Coalition must be willing to negotiate numbers, if necessary, to give union leaders the necessary tools with which to defend themselves.

SPECIFIC CRAFT PROBLEMS AND COMPLEXITIES

The problems and their peculiar complexities which will be faced by any voluntary plan staff are perhaps best illustrated through examination of some of those with which the Indianapolis Plan has had to deal.

National Ironworkers and Employers Training Program

When negotiations of the supplemental agreements were begun, the ironworkers were reluctant to discuss numbers or any other specific commitment, since the International was working on a nationwide training program which was specifically for minorities. The program planned to train 500 minorities under a Department of Labor grant, and the local argued that this should satisfy its Indianapolis commitment. The Coalition/staff members, however, refused to accept such an argument, for an effort to train 500 minorities nationwide as ironworkers would result in only two or three placements in Indianapolis. Such programs, the staff felt, could and should be considered as part of the union's efforts, but in no way should it constitute total satisfaction of equal employment requirements.

Negotiations stalemated early with little hope of compromise. Herman Walker requested advice from the Department of Labor as to what to do about the union's national program. The request brought a letter from the Secretary of Labor's office which acknowledged existence of the program, but which also affirmed the staff's view that local unions would not be able to satisfy their affirmation action obligations solely by participation in the program.[142]

Before meeting with the ironworkers' local to discuss the situation, Walker was appointed by the Office of National Projects as a nonvoting member of the Indianapolis Plan Administrative Committee for the ironworkers' program. Despite grave doubts that the national program would ever place the numbers of minorities which he had in mind, Walker agreed to let the program function temporarily as the local's substitute for a supplemental agreement.[143]

Under the leadership of the local's project director, Earl Byrne, the union accepted eleven minorities into the program during the first month of its operation and another four shortly thereafter. Walker was encouraged by the progress and allowed the program to satisfy the affirmative action commitment under the Plan. No separate supplemental agreement was ever signed. Byrne and Walker informally agreed to work toward a goal of forty placements by the end of 1971, but that goal was exceeded, with forty-seven minorities being placed in the program.[144] The forty-seven jobs for minorities represented the largest such figure for any of the crafts participating in the Plan and made this craft one of the two found in compliance by the reviewing authorities in 1972.[145]

The Administrative Committee of the ironworkers' program functions as does the operations committee in any other craft; and it is perhaps the only one which approximates the operations of the committees as initially designed under the Indianapolis

---

[142] Letter from James D. Hodgson, Secretary of Labor, to Herman Walker, July 23, 1970.

[143] Interview with Earl Byrne, Local Project Director of the National Ironworkers and Employers Training Program, July 27, 1971.

[144] IPEE Monthly Progress Report, December 31, 1971.

[145] Report of OFCC Representative Jim Wardlaw to the IPEE Administrative Committee, March 17, 1972.

Plan. It is quite active in the process of screening and interviewing prospective candidates for the program. Byrne performs similar functions to those of IPEE staff members, maintaining individual records on each minority and keeping track of their work and employers. He also notifies the Plan when minorities switch jobs or job sites, thus saving them much of the work over this particular craft.

Byrne's position is one that has not been approved by all of his fellow union workers. Prior to taking this post, Byrne was a journeyman ironworker in the local and had indirectly helped the first minority obtain a permit from the union. Many of the union members, he feels, thought the program was "a trumped-up project to get minorities their book in six months," [146] but time and actual events have dispelled that notion. Opposition will continue, he notes, as long as men are on the bench and observe minorities being hired for jobs they feel should be theirs.

The training program formally embraces the trainee and advanced trainee concepts, providing individual training manuals specifically for each. Classes are held two nights each week at a local vocational school, and they are taught by a black instructor who also teaches in the Indianapolis public schools. The contractor-chairman of the ironworkers' Administrative Committee has attended some of the classes to obtain a firsthand view of the situation, thus displaying an interest or concern not often found in the other crafts.[147]

The ironworkers still maintain their apprenticeship program, and eight of the forty-seven minorities placed in the craft are among those enrolled. This, of course, is the route that the union's president prefers to have them follow. Permission was secured by the president from the International to waive age requirements for admission to the program in an effort to channel potential applicants through the joint apprenticeship committee instead of the national training program.[148] However, Byrne has been able to continue emphasis on the trainee and advanced trainee categories.

The fact that Byrne is paid by the International out of funds provided for the training program, and thereby remains independent of the politics of the local, explains in large measure

---

[146] Byrne interview, *Op. cit.*

[147] Interview with Joe Koenig, July 19, 1971.

[148] Statement made to ironworkers' Administrative Committee, July 19, 1971, by the President, Ironworkers Local #22.

the success achieved by the ironworkers in placing minorities. Success also stems from the flexibility of Walker and the Coalition in accepting a solution which does not adhere to preconceived notions of how compliance can be achieved.

The Carpenters

It has already been pointed out that the carpenters' union delayed formal participation in the Plan for more than a year, and it would take such staunch resistance of only a few other crafts to make voluntarism unworkable. The opposition from the carpenters, however, did not surface immediately; in fact, the Carpenters' District Council President, Wendell Vandivier, was instrumental in persuading union leaders to participate in the discussions which led to the Memorandum of Understanding. The final draft of that document displeased Vandivier because of the mention of goals which he felt constituted an illegal quota. His objection was overriden by the Building Trades Council.

The carpenters' operations committee reached an early tentative agreement calling for the placement of ninety minorities each year. Vandivier, who also serves as the Apprenticeship Coordinator for the craft, attended the committee meetings as an interested party and voiced support for increased minority participation in the industry, but only if it were accomplished via the apprenticeship route. The two union representatives on the committee, however, agreed to establish the trainee and advanced trainee categories over Vandivier's dissent and the agreement was sent to the District Council for approval. On the day appointed for the signing ceremonies, Vandivier informed the IPEE that because of the death of one of the representatives on the committee, there would be a delay until a successor could be appointed. Since he personally was not on the committee, Vandivier claimed he was not eligible to sign on behalf of the craft, but he reaffirmed his support of the agreement and the craft's intention to sign.

In the meantime, the District Council had been advised by the International against signing because the carpenters' apprenticeship program was already committed to a nondiscriminatory policy.[149] That same letter also advised against agreeing to any specific percentage commitment. During the ensuing months the IPEE tried several alternatives to bring about agreement. The

---

[149] Letter to Wendell Vandivier from C.A. Shuey, dated June 17, 1970.

IPEE offered to omit mention of an overall goal of 25 percent, and then offered to meet with carpenters' representatives in San Francisco at their national convention, but the efforts were to no avail. Help was also sought from the local Bureau of Apprenticeship Training and from the Office of National Projects in Washington, but neither was able to offer a remedy.

The union presented the Plan with a revised agreement, which, the union claims, the Department of Labor helped to draft. No mention of trainees and advanced trainees was made in the proposal, which called for the creation of only thirty-five jobs. In addition, the Coalition/staff was to agree to help contractors secure federal contracts which had been going to non-union contractors. The IPEE wanted to avoid becoming actively involved in this area, for as the staff saw it, the union wanted the IPEE to do what they themselves had not been able to do.[150]

The union wanted no part of the parallel structure, sought by the staff, which would establish trainee and advanced trainee classifications. In Vandivier's words, "The trainee status threatens to tear down everything we have tried to build." [151] The apprenticeship route which Vandivier favored included a preapprenticeship program lasting six weeks and without pay to participants.[152] The program was viewed by the IPEE as discriminatory and unacceptable chiefly because of the no-pay provision.

As demonstrated previously, the contractors on the committee displayed little initiative; they merely observed the struggle between the union and the Coalition. No attempt at mediation was made, and their only active role appears to have come with the union's request that the staff help contractors, a proposal which they favored and sought to have accepted.

The staff countered the union's proposal with a revised plan, copies of which were sent to Washington. At the same time, they issued a press release stating that the carpenters were the only nonparticipating craft in the Plan.[153] The union bitterly attacked these tactics and accused the IPEE of propagandizing. Adding to the ill feelings during this period was the union's refusal to give permits to five minorities working on a

---

150 Interview with Herman Walker, July 14, 1971.

151 Interview with Wendell Vandivier, October 15, 1971.

152 *Ibid.*

153 Indianapolis Plan News Release, November 2, 1970.

Model Cities project in the city. The union claimed that none of them applied while the IPEE charged that they were never asked to apply. It was a difficult way to learn, but the staff found that it had to carry people and papers through the red tape if it were to succeed; it had chosen to play within the existing framework, and it had no choice but to comply with those procedures.

The series of delays and the surfacing of bitter feelings almost ended negotiations with the craft permanently. Walker requested help from government agencies in Washington to settle the question;[154] however, he received no reply and negotiations came to a standstill. A compliance check made by HEW some months later led to the postponement of a major construction site and an agreement followed.

While the craft did come to terms with the Plan, some compromises were made to appease their fears, chief among them the use special and second-year apprentice classifications instead of trainees and advanced trainees. But more problems arose. The union administered a series of tests which the staff thought illegal because the tests were designed to evaluate applicants after taking the basic skills course, not to screen applicants for the course. Dissention between the union and the Plan arose over the proposed training for the minorities, since the training program spelled out in the supplemental agreement had not then been initiated and the union wanted the applicants to follow the apprenticeship route. Walker threatened the craft with an imposed plan for lack of good faith effort, but before any further developments could transpire, he resigned to become the equal employment officer in the state office of the Department of Housing and Urban Development.

What followed is as yet unexplained, but within three weeks the union had its proposed training program ready and the first enrollees, all black, were soon in classes. The struggle between the staff and the union had degenerated into a personality contest which was solved only by the departure of Walker. It should be noted that the craft's (or Vandivier's) opposition did not appear to be racially motivated. This is substantiated by Vandivier's past record of interest in minority hiring. Vandivier's concern was more personal; he was attempting to protect an apprenticeship program that he had developed and

---

[154] Telegram to HEW, HUD, and DOL dated January 19, 1971, from Herman Walker, IPEE.

which he claims has been used by the International as a model for the nation.[155] He sensed that it was threatened by the parallel structure and reacted accordingly. Although a workable understanding has finally emerged, the carpenters' negotiations demonstrate some of the pitfalls which the parties should avoid.

Bid Conditions

On September 9, 1971, the Department of Labor issued an order containing bid conditions setting forth affirmative action requirements for all nonexempt federal and federally assisted construction contracts to be awarded in Marion County (Indianapolis), Indiana. The bid conditions contain two parts: Part I incorporates provisions of the Indianapolis Plan and Part II sets forth an affirmative action program applicable to those in the trades who "(1) are not or hereafter cease to be signatories to the Indianapolis Plan referred to in Part I; (2) are signatories to the Indianapolis Plan but are not parties to collective bargaining agreements; (3) are signatories to the Indianapolis Plan but are parties to collective bargaining agreements with labor organizations who are not or hereafter cease to be signatories to the Indianapolis Plan; (4) are signatories to the Indianapolis Plan but as to which no specific commitment to goals of minority manpower utilization by labor organizations have been executed pursuant to the Indianapolis Plan; or (5) are no longer participating in an affirmative action plan acceptable to the Director, OFCC, including the Indianapolis Plan." [156] Theoretically, the bid conditions were issued as a further inducement for parties to participate in good faith with the voluntary Indianapolis Plan. In the event that the parties do not choose such participation, Part II clearly specifies an imposed plan as the alternative with stated ranges of minority manpower utilization by craft expressed in percentage terms.

Unfortunately, the staff of the Indianapolis Plan did not participate in developing the bid conditions nor were they formally

---

[155] Vandivier interview, *op. cit.*

[156] *Order:* To Heads of All Agencies, from James D. Hodgson, Secretary of Labor, Arthur A. Fletcher, Assistant Secretary for Employment Standards, and John L. Wilks, Director, Office of Federal Contract Compliance, dated September 9, 1971.

notified of their initial publication. In fact, the bid conditions reflect little or no understanding of the Indianapolis construction situation. This has led to difficulties in the administration of the Plan.

Requirements of the Part II bid conditions, for the most part, were more strict than the goals of the voluntary plan as negotiated the year before. Several crafts (carpenters, cement masons, and tile and marble setters), however, were not specifically mentioned in the proposal and, in some cases, the goals were considerably less than those agreed to by the crafts in the supplemental agreements. This was particularly true for the electricians and the operating engineers. Omission of the cement masons was understandable since the union membership is almost 70 percent black; but to exclude the carpenters, especially following the incidents related in the previous section, is beyond comprehension.

The goals established for the electricians and operating engineers presented a difficult situation. When the bid conditions were issued, both crafts were committed to a 15 to 20 percent minority representation in the craft after five years. The bid conditions lowered those goals for the electricians to a 6.6 to 7.8 percent range and to a 7.7 to 8.8 percent range for the operating engineers.

The bid conditions were issued, and later discovered by the staff of the Indianapolis Plan, at a time when goals and supplemental agreements were being negotiated for the remaining three years under the Plan. Since Part II of the bid conditions contained lower requirements for some of the crafts, the staff would have been in a difficult position if the parties had known about the goals in Part II and decided to use them in negotiations. Introduction of the goals in Part II would have opened the problem of how the percentages were determined.[157] The

---

[157] The problem of developing realistic goals in imposed plans is further highlighted in the following announcement by the Department of Labor: "Sidestepping potential political embarrassment, the Labor Department's Office of Federal Contract Compliance (OFCC) has quietly abandoned its efforts to impose a Newark plan for minority hiring in New Jersey. Federal officials this week notified civil rights officials in Newark that there would be no federal plan imposed on the area. The OFCC decision came after local officials pointed out that the mandatory goals and timetables for minority hiring proposed under the federal plan were substantially weaker than the quotas already agreed to voluntarily by contractors, unions and civil rights groups in the area." (*Engineers News Record*, August 10, 1972, p. 7)

staff had no part in developing the figures and were not in a position to explain or defend them.

Negotiations by the Plan proceeded as if the bid conditions had not been issued, and no mention of them was made during the discussions of new agreements. Whether the crafts knew of the bid conditions is still not known, although the electricians held out longer than any other craft and forced a substantial compromise in the numerical goals. The IPEE staff did not want the union to be in the position of successfully opposing the Plan, which would have happened if the craft had refused to sign and then been placed under the more lenient bid conditions.

Although the figures proposed under the bid conditions were not coordinated with the Plan, their intention of producing jobs for minorities in the nonunion sector can be an effective supplement to the existing voluntary plan if minorities are to gain employment in the entire industry. The two sets of requirements must work together and not create conflict, if minorities are to find opportunities in the nonunion as well as the union sector in construction.

If nonunion contractors sign agreements with the Plan in order to avoid the more severe requirements of the bid conditions, the work of the staff of the Indianapolis Plan will increase significantly. Not only is the nonunion sector less organized from the standpoint of craft and contractor associations; it also covers a much larger job territory in the residential areas. Given the staff's current policies, it is extremely doubtful that sufficient attention could be devoted to both areas without a substantial increase in manpower. The staff is trying to cope with both areas, but once construction activity picks up, it is unlikely that they will be able to deal with the entire area as effectively as they have the smaller commercial sector.

FEDERAL AGENCY REVIEW

The first formal review of the Indianapolis Plan was initiated by the Department of Labor in January 1972. A team of compliance officials and other government representatives from various agencies visited the city in January and March to determine how many minorities of those claimed as placements were still on the job and to review the individual craft situations with each operations committee.

The January visit lasted five days while the reviewing team visited the Plan's offices and numerous construction sites in an effort to locate and talk to minorities who had been placed by the Plan. Several men were interviewed who were either laid off but still active in the Plan or who were listed as having quit. If personal contact with the individuals was not possible, an effort was made to locate them by phone.

At the end of the year 1971, the Indianapolis Plan had claimed credit for some 300 placements, but the reviewing team could only find 110 minorities on the job. The fact that it was January and the nadir of the construction season partially accounts for this lower figure; nevertheless, the findings indicate that many people have not stayed with the jobs once placed. The staff has found that some participants in the Plan look upon their job as a short-run, money-making opportunity. Despite their efforts to select and place only those who appear to be genuinely interested in a career in construction, the staff knows that some will drop out or misuse the opportunity.

A second review of the Plan in March to determine the reasons for noncompliance in particular crafts yielded the following results: the ironworkers and roofers were found to be in compliance; it was recommended that the bricklayers, tile and marble setters, and elevator constructors be placed under bid requirements established for Indianapolis in September 1971 for crafts not fully participating in the voluntary plan; and the remaining crafts were placed on probation until June 1972.

This federal action brought immediate response from the crafts. Within one week after the March meetings, the crafts placed on probation began to react, largely as a result of the contractors having finally seized the initiative. A new contractor representative on the carpenters' operations committee, for example, convened the committee and developed a proposal for two minority apprenticeship classes, one to start in April with fifteen men, the other in June with twenty. In addition, the committee agreed to place forty-five minorities by the fall of 1972. The electricians placed three men within a week after the review and five more in April; however, in that particular craft, all jounreymen were off the bench by the first of April and travelers were being used to fill openings.[158] In an effort to be removed from the noncompliance list, the elevator constructors placed two men in the week after the review.

---

[158] Conversation with Albert Butler, April 14, 1972.

In anticipation of the proposed completion of the Plan's audit in June 1972, the staff and committees in Indianapolis prepared information relevant to particular craft situations to be presented to OFCC. Much to their dismay, however, the staff was notified that the audit would not be completed as scheduled and that a report had been sent to Washington indicating that nine trades— asbestos workers, carpenters, elevator constructors, pipefitters, plasterers, tile and marble setters, brick masons, sheet metal workers, and operating engineers—were in noncompliance and should be moved from Part I to Part II of the bid conditions for Marion County. Since the Plan's contract was to expire in August, with refunding contingent upon the OFCC's recommendation, the staff was discouraged that a final review would not be made. Funding for only eight of the seventeen crafts would be a serious curtailment of the Plan's activities and those crafts that had worked to be removed from the March probationary status were greatly demoralized in view of the following facts: [159]

Elevator Constructors: As of July 21, 1972, the Plan placed fourteen men; this number exceeds the requirement under Part II of the bid conditions by four.

Operating Engineers: As of July 10, 1972, the Plan had placed thirty-one men; thirty-two would be required under Part II of the bid conditions; as of August 4, 1972, seven other men were being processed for placement.

Pipefitters: As of July 10, 1972, forty-seven men were placed; under the bid conditions, only thirty-three are required.

Tile and Marble Setters: Ten placements have been made; ten placements are required under Part II bid conditions.

Carpenters: The carpenters have resolved their problems and trainees or special apprentices make up a good portion of the fifty-six placements made in that craft; as a result of the March review, the carpenters' goal for 1972 was readjusted to eighty.

[159] Letter from the IPEE Staff, August 4, 1972.

Bricklayers and Plasterers:	Both crafts have lost membership over the past few years. The Plan has put little emphasis on placing new minority bricklayers because when the Plan started there were several minority journeyman bricklayers who were on the bench. The Plan's efforts were directed toward rehiring minorities who were already in the trade instead of flooding the industry with minorities who would have little chance to work in the future.
Sheet Metal Workers:	The sheet metal workers' trainee program was not instituted until February 1972; eleven of the seventeen placements in the craft have been made in 1972, indicating some progress in the craft.

It is not surprising, in view of the foregoing facts, that the Plan's staff and its committees have recommended strongly that the audit be completed before any final determination as to compliance and funding is made.

During the reviews of the Indianapolis Plan, it became obvious to representatives of the federal agencies which funded housing and small commercial projects that their departments had not been awarding contracts on the basis of actual compliance with the Plan. This was particularly true in the nonunion sector, where contractors in submitting bids indicated participation in the Indianapolis Plan as their affirmative action program. The awarding agencies, not knowing otherwise, accepted this, and contracts were awarded to these contractors.

As noted earlier, there are few nonunion contractors participating in the Plan. The presence of the nonunion contractors association had done more to disrupt than help proceedings, and it was asked to leave, thereby making the Plan an essentially union-oriented project. Few of the agencies, on the other hand, knew of this and were accepting the statements of the contractors who claimed participation in the Plan.

To correct that situation, the staff of the Plan is attempting to compile and make available to those federal agencies a list of all participating contractors, against which claims of participation can be verified. Without that information, these agencies would probably be unable to identify contractors who have not hired minorities but who have arranged to find a third alternative, between the Plan and the bid conditions, which is not supposed to exist.

THE NONUNION SECTOR

Because of their immense size and lack of organization, contractors and crafts in the nonunion sector present a strong contrast to the union sector. Operating basically in the residential areas, but with a foothold in small commercial work, individual nonunion contractors are generally either heavily involved in federal work or not at all.[160] Most of the contractors belong to or are affiliated with the local subsidiary of the National Association of Homebuilders, the Building Association of Greater Indianapolis (BAGI), and through BAGI participated indirectly in the early planning sessions of the Indianapolis Plan. During the two years that the Plan has been operating, nonunion contractors have had little formal contact with it. A few contractors have chosen to sign an agreement with the Plan on their own.

The imposition of bid conditions, however, draws the nonunion contractors back under the umbrella of minority hiring plans, for they must either join the Plan or face the requirements of the bid conditions. According to BAGI Executive Secretary, Richard Jones, the nonunion sector has many more minorities in its labor force than does the union one. This situation exists because of the traditional lack of formal exclusionary policies in residential work.[161] The concentration of minorities in the unskilled trades is still evident, although there are minority journeymen in almost every craft.[162] In fact, the unions have tried unsuccessfully to lure nonunion blacks into their membership in order to boost their performance record under the Plan.

Jones notes that the association foresaw the minority problem several years ago and decided to try to develop formal training programs by craft which would focus on residential work, and through which the industry could attract trained minorities. Some opposition was raised by contractors because of the lack of de-

---

[160] Interviews with Richard Jones, executive secretary, Building Association of Greater Indianapolis, October 15, 1971, and Malone Zimmerman, general contractor, January 17, 1972.

[161] Jones interview, *op. cit.*

[162] *Ibid.*

finitive craft lines in this sector, which permits carpenters to perform some masonry work, for instance, or allows painters to plaster if necessary. The contractors did not wish to narrow the scope of work and sacrifice economic advantages arising from a flexible use of construction workers.

The first apprenticeship program which BAGI initiated was for carpenters, by far the largest individual craft in this sector, accounting for 35 to 40 percent of the workers, according to one contractor.[163] The program began well and included minorities in each of the first few classes. Since most of the entrants quit the program after one year, it never progressed to third and fourth year training.[164]

One of those asked to participate in the supervision of the program two years ago was Malone Zimmerman, a minority contractor who was active in seeking out minorities for the industry. Zimmerman reorganized the program, altered the scheduled training, and built a classroom in his office in which to hold classes. Since becoming involved with the carpentry program, Zimmerman has succeeded in establishing similar programs for plumbers, electricians, painters, and masons. While he admits that the nonunion sector is far from attaining the organization and proficiency of training that characterizes that of the union sector in construction, he feels the gap is being closed.

One unusual thing about the five nonunion training programs is that entrance requirements have been made as liberal as the Bureau of Apprenticeship and Training would allow. In the carpentry program, for instance, there is no subject matter or educational grade level requirement; only an ability to read and write is necessary.[165] Zimmerman claims that BAT delayed approval for more than a year and a half; he believes that approval came only with a push by the National Association of Home Builders.[166] The recently approved plumbing program which requires two years of high school, took nine months of negotiations before BAT approval was granted.[167]

The residential contractors have begun to move into small commercial work once done by union workers. The competition of

---

[163] Zimmerman interview, *op. cit.*

[164] *Ibid.*

[165] "Standards of Apprenticeship for Carpenters," BAGI Training Program, 1971, p. 4.

[166] Zimmerman interview, *op. cit.*

[167] *Ibid.*

lower wages and greater production was instrumental in this change. The unions now are beginning to counter that push by negotiating residential wage agreements which establish a union wage rate only a few cents over the nonunion scale. They argue that for the extra cost the contractors can be assured of qualified journeyman work. The IPEE staff has watched this struggle from a distance and with mixed emotions; but since the Plan mainly covers union contractors, they look favorably on the expansion of union jobs, which means more work for minorities.

The question of bid conditions, as discussed previously, has brought the unorganized sector within the framework of planning for increased minority hiring, although as of April 1972 there had been little rush to join the Plan. According to the Plan's director, most contractors have been working under the bid conditions, which have not yet been applied very stringently.[168]

OTHER TRAINING AND UPGRADING PROGRAMS

In addition to the numerous craft-oriented training programs which have been discussed in this study, several other more basic programs are being tested in the Indianapolis public schools through the aid of unions and contractors alike. The schools have been the target of several union recruiting programs in the last few years, but they have not produced many applicants. This situation might be attributed to the traditional exclusionary practices of the industry, which are still foremost in the minds of the students.[169]

One program currently being tested in three city schools is a required construction course for seventh and ninth graders. Funded by the Department of Labor, the program has also received gifts from the Associated General Contractors for the training of additional teachers. In a sense, this type of training combats the minority problems from another direction, attempting to familiarize the students with the various crafts and to develop the necessary basic skills.

Another similar program is being conducted in the city's high schools; there is hope that on-the-job training will be available to supplement the classroom sessions, and the unions participating may offer credit toward the apprentice training if all goes as planned.[170]

---

[168] Interview with Albert Butler, April 14, 1972.

[169] Vandivier interview, *op. cit.*

[170] Interview with Edward Harding, Building Contractors Association, June 24, 1971.

JOBS-70

The Department of Labor's JOBS-70 program has had no positive effect on aiding minorities to secure work in the construction industry in Indianapolis, and the one major project in which it was used turned most local supporters of the Plan against it.

In 1970, Boise-Cascade entered into a JOBS-70 program for a development on the east side of the city, and as required, secured from each subcontractor a commitment to hire and retain a specific number of minorities, collectively totalling in excess of thirty. The minorities were recruited from the immediate locale and put to work in the various trades. However, problems developed over the training which each minority was supposed to receive, as no plans had been made in advance. When Indianapolis Plan officials visited the site, they found some men being taught courses in fence erection and installation of aluminum siding and operating engineer candidates driving bulldozers around local side streets.

At the conclusion of the work for each subcontractor, the minorities hired for the project were laid off and that was the extent of their training and employment. This action left a bitter feeling among local officials and community leaders who had initially pushed for such a project. They were so bitter, in fact, that they recommended the refusal of a JOBS-70 proposal by a nonunion minority contractor who was willing to "go union" and hire twenty minorities to begin work at Camp Aterbury near the city.

Subsequent to the Boise-Cascade incident, minorities who had been employed and laid off were referred back to the Indianapolis Plan for placement, adding to the pool of available but unemployed instead of the employed workers. The second JOBS-70 project had the staff's approval as it had twenty minorities ready to put on the job at any time. However, the state Employment Security Commission wanted to fill some of the slots and the staff agreed to divide the twenty placements. Unions argued against the project on the basis of reverse discrimination, noting that they had men on the bench who had a first claim to the jobs, if they were union jobs. In addition, there could be no more than one trainee per four or five journeymen, meaning four minority trainees, at most, could be hired. The squabble between placement agencies and between the unions and the contractor over hiring policy left the proposal in a state of disarray.

CHAPTER X

Voluntary Plans:
Implications and Recommendations

The Department of Labor has recently announced that it intends to initiate and fund additional voluntary plans in 1972. The Indianapolis Plan affords valuable insights into the characteristics of an operational voluntary plan. Assuredly, neither the government nor any two of the three local participants alone can make it work, for it requires a total effort and maximum cooperation to implement a voluntary plan. The government can, however, provide a sound base around which the plans can be built, and this should be a part of its responsibility at the outset.

THE GOVERNMENT'S ROLE

An active role by the government is crucial if voluntarism is to be anything other than a precursor to failure. Experience under the Indianapolis Plan offers federal agencies several examples of what not to do or expect, and it further demonstrates what can be accomplished when people are dedicated to solving local problems. Government action should be directed in an unobtrusive manner toward providing the necessary tools with which the staffs of the plans will operate. At the same time, the government must indicate clearly to the participants that results are expected and that the Plan will be carefully monitored.

The term "voluntary" as applied to the plans is quite obviously a misnomer. It is unrealistic to believe that local union leaders will circumvent the power structure or that contractors, especially those in marginal situations, will act in a manner that may endanger their status with the union, each for the purpose of achieving a better racial balance in the industry. Therefore, government policy must be forceful enough to coerce both unions and contractors into "volunteering," and then it must occasionally nudge them, as was done in the OFCC review in Indianapolis, to make sure that they continue to "volunteer." Obviously, the penalties of an imposed plan must be severe for both unions and contractors if they are to choose voluntarism.

Few contractors can sustain themselves if disbarred, and few unions want to see their control of the labor supply threatened. The mid-American fear of big government is strong in Indianapolis, and the Coalition wisely, and perhaps unknowingly, seized upon it in threatening from the beginning to ask for intervention.

ADMINISTRATIVE ORGANIZATION AND PROBLEMS

Sound administrative organization is an important feature of a successful voluntary plan. Unfortunately, few voluntary plans have lasted long enough to develop strong internal procedures. The development of detailed personnel files and follow-up procedures provides an excellent starting point for any voluntary plan.

Few staffs are able to function immediately in an effective manner, and the Indianapolis experience sheds light on additional needs which early action by the government might satisfy. The staff of the Indianapolis Plan was not appointed until late in June, two months after the negotiations of the supplemental agreements had begun. Unless a staff is appointed from those intimately involved with the various functions of the Plan, such as the operations committees, it will be entering the situation without the necessary experience for immediate implementation. This reflects the importance of personalities, and it demonstrates the need to cultivate working relationships in the early stages. Coalition or community representatives, who have worked closely with the plan from the outset, should be encouraged to continue in their capacities as members of the staff. The community may then want to choose its negotiators in the beginning with the idea that if the proceedings go well, those who enter early will have the opportunity to remain.

The uniformity and coordination which derives as a result of the same four minority members sitting on each of the operations committees is another feature of the Indianapolis Plan of which other plans should be aware. The experiences of the Indianapolis Plan also show the value of having the staff offices in an accessible location and the need to demonstrate a personal interest in the applicants.

CONCEPTS AND FLEXIBILITY

Other voluntary plans can benefit from the invaluable lessons which coalition bargainers learned in negotiations with the crafts in Indianapolis. There are certain advantages for both unions and contractors in voluntarism, and they must be emphasized to encourage a plan's development. Among these is the assurance that a demonstrated good faith effort, which includes active participation in a voluntary plan, satisfies equal employment requirements of the law, and that goals are more flexible and sensitive to local conditions when determined there and not in Washington. Arguments about the use of trainee and advanced trainee classifications can be avoided in the future by reference to the Indianapolis Plan, where, after a year's discussion, the use of special and second-year apprentice titles were agreed upon by the Carpenters. Negotiations in other cities can now point to the foregoing as an example or precedent.

The classifications of trainee and advanced trainee are perhaps the most important contributions put forth under voluntarism, since they establish a parallel structure for training minority workers for the construction industry. As an alternative to the traditionally closed apprenticeship routes, these two new job classifications have enabled minorities to break down the first barrier of getting onto the job sites, and they are enabling those workers to begin to develop the necessary credentials to break the second barrier of getting into the unions as full-fledged members. If every apprentice class for two years was composed only of minorities, there still would not be a sufficient number of minorities available to contractors to meet equal employment requirements; hence, the apprenticeship route is only an adjunct to the structure as put forth here. At the same time, most minorities will need classroom training in excess of that required for apprentices, both in their skilled field and in basic math and English subjects. This is a most vital service which the staffs of voluntary plans must coordinate and provide.

It is equally important that the implementation of a voluntary plan be handled in such a manner that it does not discourage potential participants before it gets started. One way, and there are others, is to do as Indianapolis did and first obtain an agreement so general that all can sign without jeopardizing individual or political aspirations, yet specific enough that it commits the parties to the overall goal. Supplemental agreements secure specific commitments and detail proposed methods of implementation. It is imperative that the staff and coalition ensure that some degree of flexibility be exercised and demonstrated in their demands and in the final solutions.

ROLE OF THE BLACK COALITION

There can be little doubt as to the significance in a voluntary plan of a strong coalition that is able to act and speak for the community. It can provide an excellent source from which to draw leaders for the plans. If the construction industry is enjoying a strong season and there is a situation of "jobs for all," then the coalition can be weaker without a substantial loss. On the other hand, as the Indianapolis Plan demonstrates, when the industry is not prospering, the coalition (through the plan's director and staff) may be called upon to exercise a more moderate approach than perhaps normally acceptable to the black community. It must be able to allay fears and quiet discontent without undermining its own support.

Since few coalitions are as strong and stable as that in Indianapolis, it must be recognized that the task of implementing voluntary plans is extremely difficult. A disorganized minority community is not likely to survive negotiations and actually produce a workable plan with the building trades unions as the theory of voluntarism would have it.

An excellent test of the coalition's ability to operate emerges in the early negotiations of the general agreement, and it should offer an insight into the future if negotiations continue into the craft-by-craft stage. Federal officials must be prepared for the plausible situation that both unions and coalitions may want the imposed plans, one for very political purposes, the other because it lacks the capability for administering the voluntary plan.

COMMUNICATION

Finally, if new plans are to benefit from experiences of their predecessors such as in Indianapolis, there must be some provision for organized presentation and exchange of information in the early stages of development. This exchange could be conducted by teams of government officials visiting the cities or teams from the cities visiting them. There is no reason why existing voluntary plans cannot serve as the basic models for shaping expansion of this approach to the integration of the construction crafts.

Voluntarism cannot be imposed by the government, but neither can it generally function without government support. Indianapolis has managed to continue operation of its Plan without a great deal of assistance from Washington. If the federal government does not intend to become closely involved in these plans, it is a mistake to establish them. The Indianapolis Plan has had an extremely diligent staff; it has also been fortunate, even lucky, with its operational and administrative successes and with the continuous strong support from the minority coalition, which has understood a slower pace of minority placements than was planned. The rare combination of factors which have produced a strong plan in Indianapolis is not available to all cities, and it would be unrealistic to expect them to operate in a similar manner without guidance.

UNION MEMBERSHIP AND THE TIME FRAME

In conclusion, when it comes to determining the success or failure of voluntarism, evaluators should refrain from using union membership as the sole criterion, since only those minorities who had prior training and experience have been eligible for membership. In the nonunion sector, where minorities have allegedly had a larger share of the work than in the organized sector, there are some who are qualified, but few who are willing to switch to the union side. As a result, only 35 to 40 qualified journeymen have been found in the Indianapolis community. However, the Coalition and IPEE staff were aware of this situation from the beginning and wisely chose to put their emphasis in the area of securing the necessary training and opportunities which would eventually qualify those being placed for union membership, a period which lasts for approximately four years, depending on the requirements of each craft.

Evaluation of the voluntary plan at an early date must consequently focus on qualitative developments in training and preparing minorities for union membership. This is why this study has emphasized strong administrative organization which must be present before the necessary coordination can be exercised or before the cooperation of other parties will be secured. Quantitative results should follow if the structure is established. This is the point which the Indianapolis Plan has now reached. The foundation has been laid, and seemingly quite well. The government has reappeared on the scene to use its influence, and a good season for the industry should produce excellent results for the Plan.

PART IV

Findings and Recommendations

CHAPTER XI

Findings and Recommendations

An examination of the findings and recommendations of the imposed and voluntary plans studied herein should bear in mind a basic underlying distinction between the two: the voluntary Indianapolis Plan was designed to place a stated number of individuals in each of the seventeen construction crafts with the belief that those who were placed would become union members and assured some continued work experience; on the other hand, the imposed, Washington Plan was developed to assure that a stated percentage of man-hours would be filled by minority members under construction contracts with no particular attention given to the individual placed and/or his employment beyond a stated contract.

The Office of Federal Contract Compliance has done an admirable job with the limited resources it possesses regarding the Washington Plan, but we think it is becoming clear that a certain amount of hometown administration is necessary for any affirmative action plan to work. The imposed plan provides the stick which is often needed to move contractors who would otherwise made no special effort to correct the exclusionary practices of the past. An imposed plan, however, raises tensions and makes agencies such as OFCC the scapegoat for union, contractor, and minority alike.

An imposed plan is not a substitute for cooperation between those who need minorities and those who know where to find qualified minority applicants. Because of the absence of such cooperation, many of the openings created by an imposed plan go unfilled and racial tensions remain high. There are cases where a contractor has job openings for minorities but does not know where to go to find qualified candidates. In other cases, community organizations which lack an understanding of the industry's requirements refer young blacks doomed to rejection. Contractors become convinced that there are not enough skilled minorities to meet the goals of the Plan. Unions claim almost universal nondiscrimination but are not trusted by the community. They too claim that there are few skilled minorities available.

A local dialogue among key representatives of government, industry, labor, and the community is needed. Each element should be able to express its needs and ask the assistance of the other. Under the umbrella of the imposed plan, unlike normal hometown solutions, the incentive to hire more minorities is realistically created by government pressure. But the recruiting, training, and placement activities, which in the end will determine the success of any plan, must be coordinated and locally administered. At present, they are fragmented and frustrating to community and industry alike in Washington.

On the other hand, hometown plans need some of the governmental pressure that accompanies imposed plans, for it is the government's action or threat of action which provides the catalyst for voluntarism. Even then, it does not guarantee cooperation between employing or hiring groups and the potential suppliers; rather, it only provides the necessary reason to bring those people together to discuss the problems and hopefully to develop some common approach to solving them. Again, OFCC must play the role of scapegoat for each of the parties.

If any of the various groups choose not to participate, then voluntarism is dead. It cannot be imposed on those who do not want it. Consequently, in this vein, the penalties of a threatened imposed plan can be neither so light that unions and contractors would opt for them nor so harsh that community leaders would prefer them. Although voluntarism cannot be imposed, it can be sold to the various potential participants, and this must be done if anything more than negative support is to be generated. That a voluntary plan is more flexible because of its adaptability to local situations is perhaps its biggest selling point, and this must be not only understood, but also believed by each group.

FINDINGS: THE WASHINGTON PLAN

Administration and Structure

1. Without the Plan, most unions and contractors would not have made much of the effort to find and place minorities that has occurred since June 1970. The Plan has successfully provoked action where voluntarism failed.

2. The communication of market needs and availability of minority manpower remains frustrated by the fragmented nature of the response to the Washington Plan. Contractors and unions often use informal hiring sources or personal contacts in the community. There should be a central contact point for the listing of openings and requirements, the matching of jobs with minority candidates, and the following up of eventual placement.

3. Few contractors, union officials, or community leaders know whom to contact to resolve problems regarding the Plan. The breakdown of communications and absence of a local administration are two weaknesses of imposed plans.

4. The estimated 12 percent growth rate per year in all trades, on which the escalating goal ranges were based, appears unrealistic in many cases. Thus, contrary to the Plan's intent, some goals could only be met by displacing existing craftsmen. Furthermore, although the Plan will allow revision of the goal ranges, none has taken place; few in the industry are aware of such a provision and have thus made no effort to utilize it.

5. A government-imposed plan was inevitable given the individuals involved and the short time available for negotiating a hometown solution. Community representatives had never successfully worked with the industry or organized labor, thus a voluntary plan would only place them at a severe disadvantage.

6. The provision in the Plan requiring contractors to report the utilization of minorities throughout their work forces—on federal and private sites—is intended to prevent the "motor-cycling" of minorities for compliance purposes. Unfortunately, private-site data reporting has caused confusion among contractors with multiple federal contracts and represents a significant weakness of the reporting system. Subcontractors are able to "motorcycle," since only the general contractor reports his total work force and the man-hours performed by subcontractors' employees on *federal* sites. Furthermore, a general contractor with several federal contracts will report the same private work to each federal agency, thus double-counting his private-site work force.

7. A comparison of the percentage of man-hours performed by minorities on federal sites and the proportion of minorities in the respective unions indicates that many trades have been able to comply with the Washington Plan goals without substantially altering the racial makeup of the unions. This suggests that much of the compliance is achieved by the judicious

placement of existing minority members and the use of permit holders, trainees, apprentices, and travelers, all of whom lack the union guarantee of continued referral once the federal project has been completed.

8. Training programs and the additional requirement that 5 percent of those working on METRO sites be local disadvantaged have enabled minority workers to win a larger part of METRO jobs, but most minorities hired are not working in the skilled trades covered by the Plan. At present most of the minorities working are in operating engineer, carpentry, laborer, tunnel, and trucking trades; thus the Washington Plan has yet to have its greatest impact on METRO employment and METRO employment has yet to have an impact on the Plan.

Community

9. Those representing community interests think that the inclusion of suburban construction work under the Plan discriminates against the inner city resident. They favor a city-only plan with goals that reflect the majority status of the minority population, i.e., goal ranges in excess of 70 percent. These leaders note that minorities have traditionally had difficulties reaching suburban work sites.

10. Many openings created by the Plan are not filled by minorities because few blacks respond to advertisements or those who do respond often fail to complete the application procedure. The Plan creates the demand but there must be a mechanism to ensure placement.

11. Most of the jobs filled by minorities because of the Plan have apprentice trainee or permit holder status. There have not been many lateral entries of minorities into the journeyman category.

12. One major factor in the low response to job openings in the community is the dirty work and exclusionary image of the construction trades.

13. The alleged pool of minority craftsmen outside of construction is smaller than envisioned and will not provide an effective source of minority manpower for Washington Plan contractors. The Plan has created demands for minority workers, but the existence of an affirmative action program alone is insufficient to change the entrenched opinion of minorities that construction is exclusionary and offers no career for them.

14. Recent revival of pressure on the METRO system should eventually have an effect on the Washington Plan. The efforts by the METRO Coalition of Concerned Citizens have brought the problems of the minority contractor to the public's attention. If successful in its attempts to win more contracts for minority firms or joint ventures with existing white contractors, this movement will result in increased minority man-hour utilization on some federal sites.

15. In general, the Washington Plan has not been enthusiastically received by the community. The Plan is not seen as an effective means of penetrating union-dominated construction. Moreover, the community has little faith that governmental regulations, no matter how good on paper, will bring true equal opportunity.

16. D.C. Vocational Schools have had little involvement with the Washington Plan and many counselors and job coordinators have not even heard of it. Vocational education suffers from the deficiencies of inferior prior education, a well-entrenched image of low quality, lack of funds, facilities and proper personnel, poor communication with the industry, curricula that are not parallel to current industry needs, and dependency on union good will for successful placement.

Contractors

17. The Plan, as amended on December 15, 1970, notes that "the prime contractor shall not be accountable for the failure of his subcontractor to fulfill his requirements; however, the prime contractor or subcontractor shall give notice to the Area Coordinator of the Office of Federal Contract Compliance . . . and the contracting agency of any refusal or failure of any subcontractor to fulfill his obligations." Unfortunately, prime contractors using customary subcontractors or those whose work on the project is crucial to the timely completion of the contract are unlikely to report a subcontractor whose debarment would prove costly.

18. Contractors agree to meet the goal minimums but rely on good faith as a safety valve if found to be not in compliance.

19. The provision that contractors are free to hire minorities directly when the union can supply none is unrealistic. Few small contractors will risk circumventing the exclusive referral agreement with their supplying unions. When a contractor is faced with debarment, the union ironically finds itself with

enhanced bargaining leverage as it deals out the available minorities.

20. Contrary to what the Plan envisioned, large numbers of black laborers are not being upgraded into the skilled ranks.

21. Although contractors generally report truthful minority man-hour data, some have been able to transfer minorities to federal sites, redesignate laborers as skilled craftsmen, and do other things to increase the reported minority man-hours.

22. The hiring of minorities by small subcontractors for a short time in order to comply on short duration subcontracts is not felt to be a major success of the Plan, unless those hired gain entrance to a union. Otherwise, once the job is complete, the minorities may be laid off. Of course, some of these minorities may gain experience that would qualify them to work on nonunion construction.

23. Most contractors are not discriminatory. Many, however, practice equal employment at their doorstep, i.e., whoever applies will be judged fairly. Because of the Plan, on the other hand, more are advertising and making special efforts to hire minorities. Many, however, still do not recognize the difference between affirmative action and nondiscrimination.

24. Our survey of union contractors indicates that the period from late 1970 through the spring of 1971 saw an increase in minority hires.

25. Small subcontractors possessing the Plan trades will most likely never comply on other than a good faith basis. Compliance for them would require discharging white craftsmen in order to place more blacks. This is prohibited by the Plan.

26. Subcontractors in the covered trades are able to shift minorities from nonreported private sites to the reported federal site and gain compliance. Contractors have admitted that compliance officials have been satisfied by the appearance of a minority on the federal site, despite his unchanged status as a member of the total work force.

27. The minority contractor will not provide a large source of minority manpower as long as the circle of "no work without experience, no experience without work" continues. Those getting contracts cannot afford to train their workers or use unproductive trainees.

28. The nonunion sector continues to be relatively uninvolved with the Washington Plan controversy. Nondiscrimination in this sector is continually taken on faith although unexamined by the

government. There is a new trend toward formal apprenticeship in the nonunion industry. Programs to recruit, train, and place minorities have been attempted but could be expanded with government pressure and/or aid.

29. The lack of craft lines in the nonunion sector enables contractors to use laborers in skilled categories for compliance purposes.

30. Our survey confirms that the proportion of minorities in nonunion construction roughly parallels their representation in the SMSA population. When broken down by skill category, however, it appears that the same patterns of concentration (in the least skilled trades) exist in the open shop as in the union shop.

31. The Washington Plan goal ranges were prepared basically from data on the union sector. Thus, the open shop must comply with goals that are not necessarily proper for their trades.

Unions

32. The carpenters were specifically excluded from the Plan although minority representation in the area's carpenters' local, by their own admission, is less than the minority population proportion in the Washington SMSA. No evidence was given by the carpenters to indicate that by 1974 the minority percentage would increase to that 26 percent level. While their apprenticeship program is quite progressive, the dropout rate of minority apprentices in that trade is about 50 percent.

33. The goal ranges for the elevator constructors, asbestos workers, lathers, boilermakers, tile and terrazzo workers, and glaziers escalate over the life of the Plan, based on the annual rate of needed replacements for these entirely different trades (12.4 percent). The plumbers and steamfitters are given the same goals although they are different unions. In short, the ranges are at best rough estimates and are surely open to criticism on grounds of fairness.

34. The Plan has been especially successful in forcing progress in previously all-white trades. The elevator constructors trade is one example. The employment of minorities remains far below that planned, but some progress has been made because of the pressure created by the Plan.

35. The sheetmetal, steamfitter, and elevator constructors trades continue to be the most recalcitrant.

36. Despite a totally exclusionary posture only a decade ago, the electrical workers have responded to demands for increased

minority participation. Since the trade requires much training, change cannot occur overnight, but the new policy is encouraging. Although the Plan has had some effect on this change, most of the progress was underway prior to June 1970.

37. Minority equal employment apprenticeship coordinators, although rare, have proved to be very successful in recruiting, counseling, and training minority union apprentices. The Electricians provide one case in point.

38. Trainees may be used to effect compliance, yet lack guaranteed entry into the union. The dropout rate is high in most preapprenticeship programs. The IBEW/NECA program, however, is unique in that government money is not used. Thus, a trainee most likely would be well counselled, for his dropping out is an expense to the union and contractors directly, not to the taxpayer. Their dropout rate has been extremely low.

39. The Plan will not make a substantial change in the racial makeup of previously all-white unions that have any degree of unemployment. As in the case of the elevator constructors, lack of employment for existing members will prevent the admission of all but helpers or permit holders, who will not displace existing members.

40. In some trades, where work is of short duration and total man-hours on federal sites are relatively few, unions and contractors will be able to effect compliance without significantly altering the racial makeup of the referral union.

Government

41. The decision as to which trades would be covered by the Plan was made from the hearings and secondary data on union membership. No evidence was presented on the racial composition of nonunion crafts, nor was an estimate of the significance of nonunion construction given to justify the exclusion of such data in the actual Plan. Moreover, many union representatives, contractors, and contractor associations did not give evidence or testimony at the hearings.

42. The man-hour reporting system which was intended to aggregate minority utilization reports from contracting agencies may not be perfected until after half of the Plan has passed.

43. Compliance inspections by contracting agencies of the federal government have been rigorous, but limited by the resources available for compliance functions. Effective compliance is even more limited by the small staff of the OFCC.

44. Compliance enforcement has varied among contracting agencies, but these inconsistencies have diminished over time as compliance officers and contractors alike become more experienced with the compliance system.

45. The government must advertise the effects of the Washington Plan to change, if possible, entrenched images of the industry. The community must see that the Plan has had success in breaking down old barriers; only then will the pool of available minorities appear. The Washington Plan Review Committee is one vehicle for winning support in the community. To date, that committee has failed to inform the community about the effects of the Plan and to become an instrument or forum for the expression of community interest.

46. As reported in the *Quarterly Review of Minority Utilization,* the percentages of minority man-hours performed in each trade comprise only that work done on federal sites. The minority utilization by contractors throughout their work force (public and private sites) is not given. Thus, we expect that the percentages are somewhat inflated by contractors who ensure that their minority employees are most visibly employed on the federal sites. Although OFCC has never claimed that these reports outline the precise performance of the Washington Plan, these percentages are in fact assumed by the public to be just that.

47. It was found that compliance can be achieved by the most white-dominated trades if man-hours reported on federal sites are the only yardstick. In June 1971, OFCC reported that of 254 man-hours of work done through April 1971 by the elevator constructors, none were performed by minorities. In September, 3,331 total man-hours and 680 minority man-hours were reported by OFCC, for work through July 1971. The new percentage was 20.4 percent which is in the middle of the goal range required by the Plan. Thus, this trade achieved overall compliance by increasing the minority utilization only 680 man-hours in one quarter. This could have been done by two men working eight and one-half forty-hour weeks. Compliance could have been accomplished without the hiring of a single minority. Similarly, the tile and terrazzo workers went from 0 percent to 68.4 percent minority with 828 minority man-hours; that could be the work of only two minorities working less than ten and one-half weeks.

48. The new apprenticeship regulations (Title 29-Part 30 of April 8, 1971) are intended to pressure unions into taking affirmative action to attract more minorities and ensure equal opportunity

for those in apprenticeship programs, but it is only conjectural at this point as to how much they will accomplish.

49. The Apprenticeship Information Center (AIC) of the District of Columbia is a valuable source of minority apprenticeship candidates. It has helped advertise construction career opportunities in the community and has tested and referred apprenticeship programs. Because of the existence of many similar organizations and training programs, such as Project BUILD, which provide competing and occasionally conflicting services, the AIC has not been able to support the Washington Plan in all trades. Successful placement is often limited by reliance on informal relationships between the AIC and the unions involved. The AIC, like others, is still only one of many fragmented groups able to assist Washington Plan contractors in meeting their goals.

Other

50. Project BUILD continues to have the greatest difficulty in placing minorities in the most skilled trades, where they are needed the most. It remains an organized and union-sanctioned program for minorities, however, and has supplied minority candidates to union contractors who are under compliance pressures.

51. Project BUILD, despite all its faults, should become an increasingly important supplier of minority apprentices because of the Washington Plan. Although resources are not available for training in all the covered trades, BUILD can provide a placement service for those unions and contractors who cooperate with it. Dropouts and quits are still a problem for BUILD and contractors and unions are still somewhat reluctant to offer total endorsement of the program. Washington Plan pressures may force a change in attitude as contractors, under fire from the government, make extra efforts to find and retain minorities.

FINDINGS: THE INDIANAPOLIS PLAN

Administration and Structure

52. Voluntarism is a tripartite function requiring the support and participation of each of the three designated parties: labor, contractors, and the community. As such, each must be capable of selecting spokesmen or representatives to put forth their ideas and negotiate agreements.

53. The formal negotiations of a plan must be conducted in such a manner as to preclude irrational and irresponsible individuals on

any side from alienating others. It may be that small subcommittees meeting in closed sessions best accomplish this necessity.

54. Voluntarism also requires philosophical and moral backing from local government administrative officials who are willing to provide the initial direction and impetus to the development of such a plan.

55. The initial agreement, which elaborates the overall goals of the Plan, was sufficiently general so as not to alienate any particular segment, yet specific enough to leave little doubt of a commitment being made.

56. Smooth transition from the general negotiations to the craft negotiations and eventually to implementation of the Plan itself is required if the initial goals of the agreement are to be carried out uniformly. Since the union and contractor members must vary according to craft on the individual operations committees, the minority community representatives are the only possible constants to insure such uniformity. The minority representatives remained involved as a group through all phases of the Plan.

57. The staff of any hometown plan must be familiar with the operations of unions and aware of the political pressures surrounding union leadership. The staff also must earn the respect of the unions and contractors in order to develop a workable relationship with some permanence. The first director of the Indianapolis staff was in the labor movement as an organizer before accepting a post in specialized education. All other staff members had labor-management backgrounds while remaining committed to the goals at hand.

58. The Indianapolis Plan director and staff are well known to each construction union by virtue of regular monthly meetings of the operations committees. Almost all contractors working in the commercial sector know the names of the director and some of the staff personnel, although not all have had regular contact with the Plan.

59. There was little administrative or procedural guidance offered or made available to the staff upon formal organization and funding of the Plan, thus forcing the staff to focus much of its initial effort on developing such procedures. This occurred at the peak of the construction season when the staff should have been able to concentrate solely on placements. The lack of help and monitoring led to several erroneous placement reports during the first year.

60. Negotiation of a supplemental agreement entails requiring a union to bargain collectively for something it does not want or

thinks unnecessary. Hence, the IPEE staff attempted to minimize this effect while remaining congnizant of union political exigencies.

61. Centralization of work records, performance reports, and worker evaluations facilitate general supervision of the Plan and will eventually eliminate one of the stumbling blocks to minority applications for union membership—the accessibility of employee records.

62. Continued followup contact with those placed by a hometown Plan is essential. It is a vital link in the destruction of the psychological barriers of closed-door policies which have become well known to the minority community.

63. The IPEE staff has demonstrated its stated goal of providing minority workers, by recommending that minority employees be laid off like any other workers if they do not perform. However, the staff has asked that they be notified first if problems develop so that counseling of the individual concerned can be made in an effort to correct the situation.

64. The Administrative Committee has been less than an activist or catalyst to the Indianapolis Plan, but not without some beneficial results. It has remained more neutral than would have been possible otherwise, indirectly maintaining that neutrality by not having to face or solve operational problems. By avoiding that, the committee has also avoided the need to take formal votes which serve to label particular people or groups and to destroy the informal atmosphere for discussion. That complacency, however, because of the extended time over which it has dominated the proceedings, will make it more difficult for the Committee to assert itself if and when it needs to act.

65. In the two years since the Plan began, 300 minorities have been placed on jobs in Indianapolis. This represents 60 percent of the commitment of 500 jobs originally planned for this period. the OFCC review in March 1972 revealed that some of the minorities were no longer in the industry.

Community

66. A minority coalition representing virtually all segments of the black community existed prior to inception of the Indianapolis Plan. Unlike those in other cities, the coalition is internally strong and speaks with a high degree of authority as the community's voice, without being undermined by dissident blacks.

67. The volatile nature of racial discrimination creates a difficult atmosphere in which voluntarism must operate. In a sense,

the community representatives have to prove themselves capable of handling the situation, by being firm in their demands for better opportunities, while demonstrating efforts to learn and help remove structural defects or individual craft problems, without appearing to bend under union opposition. There were no immediate demands of mass hirings of "faces" or displacement of whites as the unions had anticipated would be forthcoming. The Coalition's request, instead, was that training and opportunity available to anyone else be made available to minorities; in other words, the Coalition sought not to overthrow the rules but rather to increase the number of players.

68. Coalition members aided the crafts in developing apprenticeship and informal training programs and in one case even agreed to forego new placements of minorities until it could find jobs for those minorities already in the union but on the bench.

69. Our research indicates that the Indianapolis Coalition was the only one of its kind that genuinely wanted the hometown plan to succeed. As such, they displayed the typical mid-American fear of government imposition or intervention, preferring instead to solve local problems on a local level.

70. Most local officials and participants in the Plan believe that they have a solution which will be reflected in hiring data resulting from an expected boom in construction during 1972. These same officials claim that the first two construction seasons under which the Plan operated have been relatively poor and do not reflect the work of IPEE staff.

Contractors

71. Contractors were represented in the initial discussions by various trade-oriented employer organizations, serving to place the negotiations at a level above those with a more emotional attachment.

72. Negotiations of supplemental agreements can make little progress without the active participation of all groups in the Plan. Contractors appear to be the most reluctant participants, fearing that they will endanger their status with either the unions or the government if they are not extremely careful.

73. There are very few minority contractors in Indianapolis. Most of them are nonunion contractors who have had little to do with the Plan to date. Only one or two have expressed any overt interest in switching to union status, and because of their

small numbers, the Indianapolis Plan staff has not concentrated much of its effort in this area.

74. Of the more than 130 contractors who have hired minorities since the Plan's beginning, the vast majority have hired only one or two minorities each, reflecting the small size of most contracting firms in Indianapolis and the poor construction seasons of the past two years.

75. Six large area contractors, who have actively participated in the Plan, account for 22 percent of all placements made under the Plan. Of the six, three are general contractors and three are specialty contractors.

Unions

76. When dealing solely with the unions, as was the case in Indianapolis, the offer or suggestion of federal contracts only to those contractors in compliance was the largest incentive possible, especially since much federal money was going to residential, nonunion contractors. The unions thus saw an opportunity to regain some of the work they have lost in the past.

77. National union training programs, designed to help minorities, seldom offer any one individual local union sufficient evidence to prove its good faith effort under the terms of a voluntary plan. However, as with the ironworkers in Indianapolis, such programs can produce acceptable results and, consequently, should not be entirely overlooked by the coalition when it negotiates a solution with each craft.

78. The traditional pattern of minorities being better represented in the trowel and laboring trades than in the truly skilled crafts is quite evident in Indianapolis. The cement masons' and laborers' unions are overwhelmingly black and the electricians, operating engineers, ironworkers, and sheet metal crafts are overwhelmingly and almost exclusively white.

79. The status of trainee and advanced trainee for minorities opens an alternate but parallel structure of training and entry into the crafts. Although such status brings none of the benefits of union membership or apprenticeship, it does enable minorities to be placed on the job sites and receive the necessary training with the union's approval. As long as contractors are required to remain in compliance, minorities will continue to hold some jobs even in periods of great layoffs.

80. Qualifications for apprentices are often much too restrictive and discriminatory for the type of work concerned. Non-

union apprenticeship programs approved by the Bureau of Apprenticeship and Training (BAT) in Indianapolis just recently have reduced or eliminated the educational requirements, but in the union sector, labor adamantly opposes such reductions.

81. The "dilution of standards" fear of the unions is a highly emotional issue which should be avoided wherever possible. The Coalition went to great efforts to circumvent the question, knowing that if angers were aroused, meaningful dialogue would cease and negotiations would succumb to heated passions. In addition, the issue was subdued in some cases in which the Coalition actually helped set up apprenticeship programs.

82. Crafts offer little resistance when work is plentiful, but become more recalcitrant in a declining job market. The skilled crafts, particularly the electrical, carpentry, operating engineer, and sheet metal trades, have been the most vocal opponents of continued placements during periods of layoffs.

83. The Ironworkers and Roofers have been the most successful of the Indianapolis crafts in meeting their goals, while the sheet metal workers and operating engineers remain the most recalcitrant.

84. Of all the crafts, the carpenters resisted formal participation in the Plan the longest, delaying more than a year. The union raised the question of the illegality of quotas and also feared dilution of apprentice and journeyman standards. At the same time, their national union recommended not signing a supplemental agreement because it was already practicing a fair employment policy. These arguments are among the strongest that proopnents of voluntarism will have to face and overcome.

85. The carpenters' union has been using skill tests as screening devices to control admission to preapprenticeship programs and thus to the union. Tests designed to be given at the completion of the introductory skills course were, in fact, given before the course began in order to weed out the unqualified. This prevented many minorities from obtaining basic skill training in the craft.

Government

86. For political reasons, union leaders were usually willing to resist openly the Coalition's demands; but when the threat of an imposed Plan was made, they usually back down quickly, choosing not to bring about a direct confrontation. The existence of government pressure, however, arms union leaders with an

acceptable shield with which to defend their actions of accepting minority training. Such pressures need to be present behind the scenes at all times if cooperation is to continue.

87. A review of voluntary plans by federal agencies is essential if participants are to be kept aware of the government's interest in the proceedings. The review of the Indianapolis Plan in early 1972 rekindled the fires under some of the unions which had fallen down in their placement performance, at a time when the new construction season was just beginning. With a projected good season forthcoming, many unions, in an effort to stave off further government intervention, have responded by offering more and better training programs for minorities. The fact that the government did not return in June 1972 to complete its review, as promised, has had a demoralizing effect.

88. Bid conditions imposed on nonparticipating contractors are necessary in order to provide for a more punitive alternative for those who fail to commit themselves voluntarily in the hometown plans. In a sense, they are a negative incentive to participate. But where the alternate penalties are less severe than the conditions prescribed under the plan, as was the case with several crafts in Indianapolis, the opposite effect occurs, encouraging crafts to choose those penalties over participation in the plan.

89. The conversion of union membership goals to man-hours worked should produce similar percentage figures, but in Indianapolis that was not the case. The lack of coordination between local and federal authorities in implementing bid conditions is a potential block to continued operations of the Plan's staff, for the Indianapolis Plan staff never received formal notification of the bid conditions and found them accidentally, just in time to incorporate them into their bargaining strategy in renegotiating supplemental agreements during the fall of 1971.

90. There appears to have been some cooperation and coordination between the Indianapolis Plan staff and local federal agencies, such as the BAT. BAT claimed that it spurred the contractors into participating by demonstrating to them the advantages of a voluntary solution over an imposed one. However, these two particular groups have had little to do with one another for over a year; BAT claims that the Plan's director has made deals in Washington of which BAT has not been told and also claims that those minority members who sat on

both operations and administrative committees were involved in a conflict-of-interest situation. Consequently, instead of working together, there is little interchange between these two agencies, yet both are involved in the same programs in the same industry.

Other

91. The JOBS-70 program has not produced any permanent jobs for minorities in the city and the future of such undertakings locally is very bleak. Among the weaknesses of the program are the provisions for training which few subcontractors are either willing or able to conduct and the guarantee of future employment, which contractors may offer as required to secure the work, but which they ignore when the work ceases.

RECOMMENDATIONS

Although many suggestions are implied in the body of this study, the following constitute what we feel to be the most salient recommendations stemming from our research. As such, they are general and should apply in most situations.

(1) *The hearings prior to formation or imposition of a plan provide an open forum for many people with different opinions and conflicting information and data.* The presentation, acceptance, and use of erroneous material, especially statistical data concerning hiring practices, membership rosters, and minority participation in the industry can lead to unrealistic goal ranges if such material is not accurate.

(2) *OFCC should survey every construction local in the area under consideration prior to hearings to obtain firsthand knowledge of the situation.* Pre-hearing activities should also include an attempt at obtaining greater union participation than currently exists in the EEO-3 reporting system. Witnesses must be told that statistics will be checked, for if the trades find that they can remove the pressure by showing superficial good faith efforts at the hearings, the hearings held elsewhere will become less valuable.

(3) *Open hearings themselves may hinder negotiations.* By their very nature, such hearings allow ill-informed and vocal individuals to make statements which may unnecessarily alienate other groups. Antiunion, anticontractor, or antiminority statements by those whose only grounds are well-worn stereotypes

preclude future bargaining. Those in charge of the hearings, whether they are OFCC representatives or local officials, must exercise some selectivity in the hearings process and grant more time to those directly involved in the construction problem. The intent of the hearings should be to spur hometown bargaining and not to provide an open forum on the subject matter. Firm criteria for excluding a craft from coverage must be established and administered fairly. The existence of a training program, for example, should not by itself constitute grounds for exclusion.

(4) *Contractors' compliance plans should be inspected rigorously at the outset of each project by OFCC or by the appropriate funding agency.* Contractors must be discouraged from agreeing to meet the plans' goals with the intention of worrying about it later. Therefore, the threat of debarment must be real; it is the strongest and best understood weapon in the government's arsenal, and few contractors are going to risk deviant action, knowing of its presence.

(5) *Compliance officers must also check contractors' company-wide compliance posture, for concentration of attention on federal sites enables contractors to utilize minorities from private sites and win compliance without hiring new employees.* Compliance checks will always be limited by the small manpower resources available to agencies such as OFCC, HUD, and HEW, but with the increasing number of imposed and hometown plans, these agencies must begin to work together and coordinate their activities to maximize limited resources.

(6) *The Department of Labor should provide greater local coordination of federally funded construction skill training or placement programs.* There is currently a proliferation of industry, union, and community programs which have the same objective but do not work together. The Apprenticeship Information Center, Project BUILD, JOBS-70, union and nonunion apprenticeship programs, and nonfederally funded programs could become far more effective if made part of a coordinated effort to place minorities under either type of plan.

(7) *The Department of Labor should examine the effectiveness of the Bureau of Apprenticeship and Training's effort to ensure that apprentice programs provide equal employment opportunity.* New affirmative action regulations can complement imposed and voluntary plans if enforced. Educational and training requirements for entry into apprentice programs are not as inflexible as some BAT and union officials view them. They

should be reviewed first to determine if all existing requirements are job related and then for particular discriminatory effects.

(8) *Vocational schools (and public school construction programs) need greater support to improve their deteriorating condition if they are to develop into a substantial source of minority manpower in the construction industry.* Such community programs are vastly understaffed, inadequately funded, and seldom utilized.

(9) *Community leaders and administrators of the plans must recognize that the highly skilled and highly paid jobs cannot be filled by dropouts or by those unwilling to commit themselves to a long period of training.* Those who refer applicants must recognize that many of the discharges or rejections of potential minority employees are not racially motivated. Consequently, there is a great need for counseling of, and follow-up contact with, minority placements. In addition, if the plans offer openings for minority applicants, then the community or administrators cannot let any openings go unfilled.

(10) *The meager participation of minority construction firms in federal construction looms as a volatile issue in its own right, especially in Washington.* The federal government should develop a policy regarding the employment of minority firms in keeping with the spirit of the plans. Existing contractors' associations should work with the minority contractors in order to allow them to enter the mainstream of the industry. Joint ventures, with the government absorbing some of the on-the-job training, appears to be the most practical way to enable minority contractors to gain experience in more sophisticated construction techniques.

(11) *Goals for the various crafts must be somewhat flexible and realistic.* The successful negotiation of goals in a voluntary situation implies flexibility and realism, but in imposed solutions the ranges are multi-year projections and thus subject to unforeseen changes. In each case, goals should be examined at least once throughout the life of the plan. In hometown situations, renegotiation of goals after a certain time frame can be specified in the very beginning under the terms of the Plan. With imposed plans, review of goals can be made a formal requirement. The Washington Plan contains such a provision, but it has not been exercised.

(12) *Recruitment, listings of job openings, training, place-ment, and follow-up in support of the plans need to be as central-ized and coordinated as possible.* Such organization permits a more effective matching of minorities to jobs and more tangible evidence of the plans' operations. The hometown solution, as described in Indianapolis, is certainly a good starting point and far better than the existing situation in Washington. This is not to preclude, however, other methods of reorganization of administrative procedures.

(13) *In evaluating these procedures and the placement process, OFCC must look at the changes in minority membership in the unions, except where the plans are geared to training individuals outside of the apprenticeship structure, such as in Indianapolis, where trainee and advanced trainees do not hold union member-ship but receive equivalent training.* After four or five years, however, the membership figures become the most significant individual measure. In Indianapolis the Plan is geared to preparing trainees for journeyman status and union member-ship. In Washington, OFCC must expedite development of a data processing system which will provide uniform quarterly statistics on the overall performance of each trade. Such reports must com-prise federal and nonfederal data to indicate overall posture in the industry and not just on the more visible federal sites. In addition, reporting formats must be made consistent from period to period and the data presented must be clearly defined as to coverage, i.e., by craft, federal site, or private site.

(14) *Both the Washington and Indianapolis Plans are pri-marily aimed at the union sector of the industry; more atten-tion must be paid to the advancement of minorities in the non-union sector.* In Washington, the nonunion sector performs the majority of all construction work; in Indianapolis it performs substantially all residential work and a small but growing part of the commercial work. Thus, in the sector where craft lines are least evident and where mobility is greatest, little effort as a result of either plan has been made to further employ-ment for minorities. The bid conditions supplementing the volun-tary plans have just begun to affect this area and are vital to expansion of opportunities for minorities in the entire industry rather than in just one segment. It is imperative, however, that goals under such complementary systems be compatible and not afford participants an undeserved choice, i.e., a choice between the lesser of two requirements.

(15) *In an imposed situation, federal agencies should explore the feasibility of using cost-plus provisions for subcontractors in the technical trades.* On-the-job training by minorities hired for the purpose of supporting the objectives of the Washington Plan could provide the training that is often impossible in all but the most profitable firms. The agencies should demand guarantees from the employer or union that those trained through the use of federal funding will be placed at the top of the contractor's permanent hiring list and/or actually granted full union membership.

(16) *The present nature of the imposed plan places most of the compliance pressure on the contractor.* Through an expanded man-hour reporting system, verification of EEO-3 reporting, and surveys of local unions by OFCC officials, unions too must be placed in the public eye.

(17) *The Washington Plan and similar imposed Plans should be retained and extended, if necessary, to meet their original objectives.* Imposed plans should not be used where voluntarism may be more productive. OFCC will have to study carefully each area before resorting to direct government involvement. OFCC will have to improve the enforcement of the Plans' requirements, yet also act quickly to develop some local administration of the Plan.

(18) *The Indianapolis Plan should be retained and adequately supported.* The OFCC should maintain close contact with the Plan and exercise leadership whenever it is needed to assist the staff of the Plan in generating activity by recalcitrant parties in a given trade.

Index

AFL, 121
AFL-CIO, 22, 24-25, 98
  See also CIO
AFL-CIO Human Resources Development Institute, 137
American Hod Carriers Union, 115
Apprenticeship and minorities, 50-59, 82-83, 110, 179-181
  See also Project BUILD
Apprenticeship Information Center (AIC), 28, 54, 94, 182
Asbestos workers
  and Indianapolis Plan, 137, 147, 160
  and Washington Plan, 44, 52-53, 179
  minority employment on federal sites, Washington, D.C., 64, 66
  racial policies, 29
Associated Builders and Contractors, Inc. (ABC), Washington chapter, 92-95
Associated General Contractors, 164

Black Panthers, 126
Boilermakers
  and Washington Plan, 44, 68, 179
Bricklayers
  and Indianapolis Plan, 134-35, 137, 149, 159-61
  racial policies, 11-12, 19-21, 24, 115, 121
Bricklayers Locals 1 and 4, 24
Brickmasons
  See Bricklayers
Builders Association of Greater Indianapolis (BAGI), 126, 128, 162-3
Building Contractors Association (Indianapolis), 124
Bundles, Don, 131, 143
Bureau of Apprenticeship and Training (BAT), 28, 110, 137, 141, 147, 154, 163
Butler, Albert, 134
Byrne, Earl, 151-2

Carpenters
  and Indianapolis Plan, 130, 132, 134-5, 147, 149, 153-7, 159-60
  and METRO employment, 59, 62

and Washington Plan, 40, 44, 179
  nonunion sector in Indianapolis, 163
  racial policies, 12-13, 19-20, 23, 115, 121
Cement finishers
  racial policies, 11-12
Cement masons
  and Indianapolis Plan, 135, 137, 147, 157
Central and Specialty Contractor Association, 123
Chicago Plan, 128
CIO
  racial policies, 121
Civil Rights Act of 1964, 29, 128
  Title VII, 87, 130
Commissioner's Council on Human Relations, 25, 29
Construction Contractors Council, 41
Contractor associations
  and Washington Plan, 88-9
  Indianapolis, 124, 126
Contractors, 3, 23
  and Indianapolis Plan, 143, 147-149, 159
  and Washington Plan, 41, 45-8, 73-6, 84
Contractors, carpentry
  and Indianapolis Plan, 149
Contractors, electrical
  and Indianapolis Plan, 148-9
  and Washington Plan, 90
Contractors, elevators
  and OIC, 79
  and Washington Plan, 91
Contractors, minority, 20
  and METRO, 85-7, 177
  and Washington Plan, 96-7, 178
Contractors, nonunion
  and Indianapolis Plan, 162
  and Washington Plan, 73, 92-6
Contractors, plumbing
  and Washington Plan, 90
Contractors, union
  and Washington Plan, 89-90
Cooper, James, 131
Craftsman Refinement Center, 102

Davis Bacon Act, 93-4

Democratic party
  Negro support in Indiana, 120
District Government Organization
  Order 125, 25
District of Columbia Apprenticeship
  Council, 28, 51
District of Columbia Manpower Ad-
  ministration, 50
Douglass, Frederick, 19

Eaton, David H., 39
Electrical trades
  racial policies, 10, 14, 19, 21, 23-4,
    30, 179-180
  See also electricians
Electricians
  and Indianapolis Plan, 135, 149,
    157-8
  and METRO employment, 62
  and Washington Plan, 44, 52, 179-
    180
  minority employment on federal
    work sites, Washington, D.C.,
    68
Elevators constructors
  and Indianapolis Plan, 159-60
  and OIC, 79
  and Washington Plan, 44, 91, 179
  minority employment on federal
    work sites, Washington, D.C.,
    64, 68, 181
Executive Order 8802, 23
Executive Order 11246, 32, 34-5, 42,
  73, 84, 128

Fletcher, Arthur A., 37

General Aptitude Test Battery
  (GATB), 54-5
Glaziers
  and Indianapolis Plan, 135, 137, 149
  and Washington Plan, 44, 52-3
  minority employment on federal
    work sites, Washington, D.C.,
    68
  racial policies, 29
Goldman, Aaron, 25
Greater Washington Central Labor
  Council, AFL-CIO, 101

Haggerty, C. J., 99
Hod carriers
  black union in Indianapolis, 115
  racial policies, 22
Holt, David, 126

IBEW, International, 24
IBEW, Local 26, 24, 79

IBEW/NECA apprenticeship program, 180
Imposed plans, 173-5
Indianapolis Black Coalition
  See Minority Coalition of Indian-
    apolis
Indianapolis, Indiana
  racial climate, 113, 116, 118-22, 127
Indianapolis Plan for Equal Employ-
    ment (IPEE)
  Administrative Committee, 130-31,
    137, 139-40, 184
  and Employment Task Force, 127
  and JOBS-70, 165
  and minority community response,
    143
  See also Minority Coalition of In-
    dianapolis
  and minority placements, 133, 135,
    137
  and National Ironworkers and Em-
    ployers Training Program,
    150-3
  and Sky Harbor Project, 133-4
  and Washington Plan; comparison
    of goals, 173
  bid requirements for nonpartici-
    pants, 134, 156-8, 160, 164
  compliance, 139, 145
  contractor response, 143, 147-9, 159
  criteria for evaluation, 6-8
  data sources, 8-9
  federal reviews, 134, 139, 158-61
  formation, 123-4
  location of data sources, 5
  operations committees, 130-1, 144-5
  overall goals and administrative or-
    ganization, 129
  placement and follow-up activities,
    142-44
  preliminary hearings, 128-9
  special classifications of construc-
    tion workers, 129-30, 146-7,
    153-4
  staff and Plan administration, 131,
    140-2, 183-4
  supplemental agreements, 132, 140-
    1, 145-7
  union response, 128, 130, 135, 146-7,
    149-56
Ironworkers
  and Indianapolis Plan, 135, 150-1,
    159
  and METRO employment, 62
  and Washington Plan, 44, 52-3

minority employment on federal work sites, Washington, D.C., 68
racial policies, 14-15
JOBS-70
and Indianapolis Plan, 165
Jones, Launcelot, 131
Jones, Richard, 162

Ku Klux Klan
in Indiana, 113, 118-9

Laborers
and METRO employment, 59
racial policies, 22
upgrading, 90
Labor unions in construction industry, 3-5
exclusionary practices, 97, 99
hiring hall arrangements, 97
minority apprentices and the Washington Plan, 50-9
minority membership, Washington, D.C., 69, 176
racial policies, 10-15, 21-30, 75, 83, 89-90, 98-100, 115, 120-21
training programs and minority employment, 28-30, 98-99, 110, 164
upgrading of minorities, Washington, D.C., 90
See also individual crafts; Indianapolis Plan; Washington Plan
Lathers
and Indianapolis Plan, 135, 137
and Washington Plan, 44, 52-53, 179
minority employment on federal work sites, Washington, D.C., 64, 68
racial policies, 29
Lathing and Plastering Contractors Association, Indianapolis, 126
Lugar, Richard, 123, 130

Manpower Report of the President, 1964, 30
Marion County Building Trades Council, 121, 124, 130, 153
Mason Contractors Association, Indianapolis, 126
Mayor's Task Force on Construction Problems, 78
Meany, George, 24
Mechanical Contractors Association, Indianapolis, 124

Mechanical trades
racial policies, 10, 14, 19-21, 24
See also individual crafts
Memorandum of Understanding, 123-4, 128-9, 131, 145-6, 153
METRO, 34, 36, 85, 86
and minority employment, 59-64, 176-7
METRO Coalition of Concerned Citizens, 86, 177
Minority Coalition of Indianapolis, 123-4, 130, 132, 139-41, 145, 50, 153-4
Minority employment in the construction industry
and apprenticeship programs, Washington, D.C., 50-59
and Indianapolis Plan, 133, 135, 137
and METRO, 59-64, 176
and minority contractors, Washington, D.C., 96, 98
history, 10-15, 19-32, 119-121
in nonunion sector, Washington, D.C., 92-96
in union sector, Washington, D.C., 75, 88-90, 98-100
on federal work sites, Washington, D.C., 64-69
Model Cities program, Indianapolis, 126, 155

NAACP, 24, 91, 118, 121
National Association of Home Builders, 126, 162-3
National Electrical Contractors Association, Indianapolis, 124
National Ironworkers and Employers Training Program, 150-153
Negro education in Indiana, 113-4, 116, 118, 121-2
Negroes in Indiana politics, 115, 120, 122

Office of Federal Contract Compliance
See listings under United States Department of Labor
O'Neill, Joe, 131
Operating engineers
and Indianapolis Plan, 133-5, 146-7, 157, 159
and METRO employment, 59, 62
and Washington Plan, 40, 44
racial policies, 12-14, 24, 30
Opportunities Industrialization Center (OIC), 78-9, 91

Painters
  and Indianapolis Plan, 137, 149
  and Washington Plan, 44, 52-3
  minority employment on federal
    work sites, Washington, D.C.,
    64, 68
  racial policies, 12-13, 20, 29
Paperhangers
  and Washington Plan, 44, 52-3
Petty, Tom, 131
Philadelphia Plan, 31, 34, 36, 48, 98,
  128
Pipefitters
  and Indianapolis Plan, 160
  and METRO employment, 62
  and Washington Plan, 44, 52
  minority employment on federal
    work sites, Washington, D.C.,
    68
  racial policies, 14
Plasterers
  and Indianapolis Plan, 160-1
  and Washington Plan, 44
  racial policies, 11-12, 24
Plumbers
  and METRO employment, 62
  and Washington Plan, 44, 52, 179
  minority employment on federal
    work sites, Washington, D.C.,
    68
  racial policies, 10, 14, 21, 23
President's Committee on Equal
  Employment Opportunity
  (PCEEO), 25
President's Committee on Fair Employment Practices, 23, 121
President's Committee on Government
  Contracts (PCGC), 24
PRIDE, Inc., 78-9
Project BUILD, 34, 41, 44, 79, 83, 91,
  101-4, 182

Republican party
  and Klu Klux Klan in Indiana, 119
  and Negro support in Indiana, 114-5
Rodmen
  and Washington Plan, 40, 44, 53
Roofers
  and Indianapolis Plan, 135, 159
Roofing Contractors Association, In-
  dianapolis, 126
Schricker, Henry, 121
Sheet Metal Contractors Association,
  Indianapolis, 124
Sheet metal workers
  and Indianapolis Plan, 135, 160-1

  and Washington Plan, 40, 44, 52,
    179
  minority employment on federal
    work sites, Washington, D.C.,
    64, 68
  racial policies, 14, 29
Sherman, Louis, 99
Sky Harbor Project, 134
Smith, Frank, 131
Solomon, Juan C., 123, 127, 130
Steamfitters
  and METRO employment, 62
  and Washington Plan, 44, 52, 179
  minority employment on federal
    work sites, Washington, D.C.,
    68
Stone and marble masons
  racial policies, 29
Strough, Walter, 124, 149

Teamsters
  and METRO employment, 59
Tile and marble setters
  and Indianapolis Plan, 157, 159-60
Tile and terrazzo workers
  and Washington Plan, 44, 179
  minority employment on federal
    work sites, Washington, D.C.,
    66, 68, 181
  racial policies, 29
Tripartitism in Indianapolis Plan,
  148-50
Trowel trades
  and community action, 90
  racial policies, 11, 20-1, 23
  See also individual crafts
Tunnelers
  and METRO employment, 59

United States
  Commission on Civil Rights, 84
  Department of Health, Education,
    and Welfare, 155
  Department of the Interior, 22
  Department of Labor, 28, 32, 110,
    164, 166
    and Indianapolis Plan, 131-2, 134,
      151
    and Washington Plan, 35-7, 39-40,
      42
    bid conditions for Indianapolis
      Plan nonparticipants, 134,
      156-8, 160, 164
    JOBS-70 program, See JOBS-70
    Manpower Administration, 101

Office of Federal Contract Compliance (OFCC)
and imposed plans, 173
and Indianapolis Plan, 139, 145, 158-62, 166
and voluntary plans, 174
and Washington Plan, 34-35, 42, 64, 74, 76-7, 84-5, 89, 104-10, 173, 181
Department of Transportation
and Washington Plan, 34, 36-7
Housing Authority, 23
Works Progress Administration (WPA), 22, 120
Urban League, 24, 33, 76, 78-9, 88, 91, 107, 126

Vandivier, Wendell, 153-5
Volpe, John, 34, 36-7
Voluntary plans, 174, 182-3

Walker, Herman, 128, 131, 134, 140-43, 151, 153, 155
Washington Area Construction Industry Task Force (WACITF), 33-4, 37-41, 76-7, 84-5, 107
Washington Area Contractors Association, 96-7
Washington Building and Construction Trades Council, 41-2, 101
Washington, D.C. municipal government
and equal employment opportunities, 25, 28
Washington Metropolitan Area Transit Authority (WMATA), 34, 36

Washington Plan
and apprenticeship, 50-9, 182
and Indianapolis Plan; comparison of goals, 173
and METRO employment, 59-64, 176-7
and Project BUILD, 44, 91, 103-4, 182
community response, 37-41, 77, 80-8, 176-7
compliance and enforcement, 74-6, 84, 104-6, 175-8, 180
contractor response, 88-90, 92-6, 177-9
criteria for evaluation, 6-8
data sources, 8-9
location of data sources, 5
long-term effects, 88-90, 94, 97
methods of evaluation, 49-50, 108-9
minority contractors, 87, 96-7, 178
minority employment on federal sites, 64-9
minority manpower supply, 80-1, 175-6
preliminary hearings, 35-40
reporting system, 108-10, 175, 181
review mechanism, 48, 106, 175
scope and goals, 40-3, 45-8, 90, 175, 179
union response, 36-7, 39-42, 98-100, 179
Washington Plan Review Committee, 48, 64, 76, 84, 88, 90, 92, 105, 107-8
Wilks, John, 34, 37

Zimmerman, Malone, 163

Racial Policies of American Industry Series

1. *The Negro in the Automobile Industry,*
   by Herbert R. Northrup.   1968. $2.50
2. *The Negro in the Aerospace Industry,*
   by Herbert R. Northrup.   1968. $2.50
3. *The Negro in the Steel Industry,* by Richard L. Rowan.   1968. $3.50
4. *The Negro in the Hotel Industry,* by Edward C. Koziara
   and Karen S. Koziara.   1968. $2.50
5. *The Negro in the Petroleum Industry,* by Carl B. King
   and Howard W. Risher, Jr.   1969. $3.50
6. *The Negro in the Rubber Tire Industry,* by Herbert R.
   Northrup and Alan B. Batchelder.   1969. $3.50
7. *The Negro in the Chemical Industry,*
   by William Howard Quay, Jr.   1969. $3.50
8. *The Negro in the Paper Industry,* by Herbert R. Northrup.   1969. $8.50
9. *The Negro in the Banking Industry,*
   by Armand J. Thieblot, Jr.   1970. $5.95
10. *The Negro in the Public Utility Industries,*
    by Bernard E. Anderson.   1970. $5.95
11. *The Negro in the Insurance Industry,* by Linda P. Fletcher.   1970. $5.95
12. *The Negro in the Meat Industry,* by Walter A. Fogel.   1970. $4.50
13. *The Negro in the Tobacco Industry,*
    by Herbert R. Northrup.   1970. $4.50
14. *The Negro in the Bituminous Coal Mining Industry,*
    by Darold T. Barnum.   1970. $4.50
15. *The Negro in the Trucking Industry,* by Richard D. Leone.   1970. $4.50
16. *The Negro in the Railroad Industry,*
    by Howard W. Risher, Jr.   1971. $5.95
17. *The Negro in the Shipbuilding Industry,* by Lester Rubin.   1970. $5.95
18. *The Negro in the Urban Transit Industry,*
    by Philip W. Jeffress.   1970. $4.50
19. *The Negro in the Lumber Industry,* by John C. Howard.   1970. $4.50
20. *The Negro in the Textile Industry,* by Richard L. Rowan.   1970. $5.95
21. *The Negro in the Drug Manufacturing Industry,*
    by F. Marion Fletcher.   1970. $5.95
22. *The Negro in the Department Store Industry,*
    by Charles R. Perry.   1971. $5.95
23. *The Negro in the Air Transport Industry,*
    by Herbert R. Northrup and others.   1971. $5.95
24. *The Negro in the Drugstore Industry,* by F. Marion Fletcher. 1971. $5.95
25. *The Negro in the Supermarket Industry,*
    by Gordon F. Bloom and F. Marion Fletcher.   1972. $5.95
26. *The Negro in the Farm Equipment and Construction
    Machinery Industry,* by Robert Ozanne.   1972. $5.95
27. *The Negro in the Electrical Manufacturing Industry,*
    by Theodore V. Purcell and Daniel P. Mulvey.   1971. $5.95
28. *The Negro in the Furniture Industry,* by William E. Fulmer.   1972. $5.95
29. *The Negro in the Longshore Industry,* by Lester Rubin
    and William S. Swift.   1973. $5.95
30. *The Negro in the Offshore Maritime Industry,*
    by William S. Swift.   1973. $5.95
31. *The Negro in the Apparel Industry,* by Elaine Gale Wrong.   1973. $5.95

Labor Relations and Public Policy Series

3. *The NLRB and the Appropriate Bargaining Unit,*
   by John E. Abodeely. 1971. $5.95
4. *The NLRB and Secondary Boycotts,* by Ralph M. Dereshinsky.
   1972. $5.95
5. *Collective Bargaining: Survival in the '70's?* Conference Proceedings,
   edited by Richard L. Rowan. 1972. $7.95
6. *Welfare and Strikes: The Use of Public Funds to Support Strikers,*
   by Armand J. Thieblot, Jr., and Ronald M. Cowin. 1972. $6.95
7. *Opening the Skilled Construction Trades to Blacks: A Study of the
   Washington and Indianapolis Plans for Minority Employment,*
   by Richard L. Rowan and Lester Rubin. 1972. $5.95

Major Industrial Research Unit Studies

No. 51   Gordon F. Bloom, F. Marion Fletcher, and Charles R. Perry, *Negro
Employment in Retail Trade: A Study of Racial Policies in the
Department Store, Drugstore, and Supermarket Industries,* Studies
of Negro Employment, Vol. VI. 1972. $12.00

No. 50   Herbert R. Northrup *et al., Negro Employment in Land and Air
Transport: A Study of Racial Policies in the Railroad, Airline,
Trucking, and Urban Transit Industries,* Studies of Negro Employ-
ment, Vol. V. 1971. $13.50

No. 49   Herbert R. Northrup, Richard L. Rowan, *et al., Negro Employment
in Southern Industry: A Study of Racial Policies in the Paper,
Lumber, Tobacco, Coal Mining, and Textile Industries,* Studies of
Negro Employment, Vol. IV. 1971. $13.50

No. 48   Bernard E. Anderson, *Negro Employment in Public Utilities: A
Study of Racial Policies in the Electric Power, Gas, and Telephone
Industries,* Studies of Negro Employment, Vol. III. 1970. $8.50

No. 47   Armand J. Thieblot, Jr., and Linda P. Fletcher, *Negro Employment
in Finance: A Study of Racial Policies in Banking and Insurance,*
Studies of Negro Employment, Vol. II. 1970. $9.50

No. 46   Herbert R. Northrup, Richard L. Rowan, *et al., Negro Employment
in Basic Industry: A Study of Racial Policies in Six Industries,*
Studies of Negro Employment, Vol. I. 1970. $15.00

No. 45   William N. Chernish, *Coalition Bargaining: A Study of Union
Tactics and Public Policy.* 1969. $7.95

No. 44   Herbert R. Northrup and Gordon R. Storholm, *Restrictive Labor
Practices in the Supermarket Industry.* 1967. $7.50

No. 43   F. Marion Fletcher, *Market Restraints in the Retail Drug Industry.*
1967. $10.00

No. 42   Michael H. Moskow, *Teachers and Unions: The Applicability of
Collective Bargaining to Public Education.* 1966. $8.50

No. 41   George M. Parks, *The Economics of Carpeting and Resilient Floor-
ing: An Evaluation and Comparison.* 1966. $5.00

No. 40   Gladys L. Palmer *et al., The Reluctant Job Changer.* 1962. $7.50

Miscellaneous Series

17. *The Carpet Industry: Present Status and Future Prospects,*
    by Robert W. Kirk. 1970. $5.95
18. *Educating the Employed Disadvantaged for Upgrading: A Report on
    Remedial Education Programs in the Paper Industry,* by Richard L.
    Rowan and Herbert R. Northrup. 1972. $5.95

Order from the Industrial Research Unit,
The Wharton School, University of Pennsylvania
Philadelphia, Pennsylvania 19104